PLACES BEYOND BELIEF

BOOK TWO OF THE ONE GIANT LEAP TRILOGY

MICHAEL K. YEN

BALBOA.PRESS

A DIVISION OF HAY HOUSE

Balboa Press books may be ordered through booksellers or by contacting:

Balboa Press
A Division of Hay House
1663 Liberty Drive
Bloomington, IN 47403
www.balboapress.com
1 (877) 407-4847

Because of the dynamic nature of the Internet, any web addresses or links contained in this book may have changed since publication and may no longer be valid. The views expressed in this work are solely those of the author and do not necessarily reflect the views of the publisher, and the publisher hereby disclaims any responsibility for them.

The author of this book does not dispense medical advice or prescribe the use of any technique as a form of treatment for physical, emotional, or medical problems without the advice of a physician, either directly or indirectly. The intent of the author is only to offer information of a general nature to help you in your quest for emotional and spiritual well-being. In the event you use any of the information in this book for yourself, which is your constitutional right, the author and the publisher assume no responsibility for your actions.

Any people depicted in stock imagery provided by Getty Images are models, and such images are being used for illustrative purposes only.
Certain stock imagery © Getty Images.

Print information available on the last page.

ISBN: 978-1-9822-4954-0 (sc)
ISBN: 978-1-9822-4956-4 (hc)
ISBN: 978-1-9822-4955-7 (e)

Library of Congress Control Number: 2020911124

Balboa Press rev. date: 08/12/2020

"There are great ideas undiscovered, breakthroughs available to those who can remove... *one of truth's protective layers...* There are places to go beyond belief... because there lies human destiny."

Neil Armstrong, Apollo 11, first moon landing's
25th anniversary speech, 1994

Contents

Foreword

Michael Yen is a man who bridges many worlds. He grew up on the streets of one of Hong Kong's toughest neighborhoods. He rose to attain positions of distinction in the United States diplomatic corps. From there he ventured into one of the most unique, esoteric niches I can imagine – studying and then practicing Jungian psychology in mainland China. The breadth of these attainments is more than most people live to experience in a single lifetime. But, to his credit and to the benefit of readers of this book, he did not stop there. He applied both his worldly knowledge and his mastery of inner psychic realms to an exploration of the paranormal – not for the purpose of titillation or mere adventure, but as part of a deep philosophical quest to understand more deeply the source of life's mysteries.

After having acquainted themselves with the literature concerning the phenomenology of out-of-body experiences (or OBEs), Michael and his lovely wife began applying techniques and found that they could successfully enter into these mysterious altered states of consciousness. These direct experiences convinced them that the conventional materialistic vision of the world, so applicable in the corridors of power or on the streets of any major city, was incomplete (at best) or, more likely, incorrect.

I am particularly intrigued by the photograph of an apparent pyramid structure, overgrown with vegetation, featured on the cover of this book. What is that about? Conventional geologists and archaeologists all seem to agree that it is a naturally formed hill with a striking, pyramid-like shape. In recent years it has become a major tourist attraction about which a Bosnian entrepreneur has created many narratives consistent with popular, New Age mythology. Proponents of these stories suggest that this hill is actually the largest and most ancient of all man-made pyramids. Apparently, a network of tunnels (or old mining shafts) has also been discovered in the area.

Michael Yen reports that he is drawn to this interesting complex because, on one vivid occasion, he found himself traveling there in lucid-dreaming state. As a Jungian, I am sure he appreciates that, whether a natural formation or a man-made structure, the Bosnian pyramid has now acquired an aura of numinosity, simply because thousands of human beings have now made it the object of their focused attention.

As a parapsychologist, myself, I find this to be an interesting case in point. Numinous locations and structures, such as ancient pyramids and temples, appear to be very attractive to both remote-viewers and out-of-body experiencers. So, it is not surprising that Michael would find himself drawn to this location. However, at the intellectual level, we are challenged to see if we can distinguish between fact and fiction. As a former diplomat, I know that Michael Yen understands very well the challenges we face in the current "post-truth" environment that has been drastically accelerated (although not actually initiated) by President Trump. Michael also writes eloquently about the sorts of archaeological hoaxes that have existed in the past resulting from pecuniary motivations.

The situation here is a riddle within a riddle (and perhaps within, yet, another riddle). Conventional researchers typically reject the findings of parapsychology, even though the empirical data supporting parapsychology is, by now, overwhelming.[1] Parapsychologists, in spite of their own fringe status within the scientific community, are nevertheless committed to the empirical methods of science and, therefore, would be inclined to accept the verdict of geologists and archaeologists that the claims regarding the Bosnian pyramids, as presented in Michael Yen's appendix to this book, represent "pseudo-archaeology". (One wonders whether these particular "experts" are of the same ilk as those who have been debunking UFO sightings for so many decades. New data, as presented in Michael Yen's epilogue, make clear how wrong they were.)

In Michael's lucid dream, in which he flew over the Bosnian pyramid complex, he saw the pyramids covered partially with gold. And, as he hovered over a pyramid, he felt a pleasant rush of energy pulse through his body. He hypothesizes that he may have been visiting those pyramids in their heyday, perhaps as long as 34,000 years ago. An alternative hypothesis would be that his lucid dream took him to a location within our shared collective consciousness filled with the thought-forms created by the thousands of spiritual wanderers who make pilgrimages to the Bosnian sites.

Since this book is the second in a planned trilogy, we will have to wait for the final outcome of the story. Michael suggests that he hopes to visit the Visoko complex in Bosnia and that there he expects to discover insights relating to letting go of the ego. I eagerly await the next volume in this trilogy; and I applaud Michael Yen as a brilliant writer and a courageous explorer of that boundary region where the depths of the human psyche touch the fascinating worlds of power and sensation.

Jeffrey Mishlove, PhD
Host and Producer
New Thinking Allowed YouTube channel

Introduction

OUR HUMBLE HOME

In *Physical to Metaphysical in Four Steps and ONE GIANT LEAP*, published in 2017, I laid out the three steps that can help the reader become aware of, and separate from, being overly identified with the physical, emotional, and intellectual aspects of being human. In the fourth step, I wrote about how we can then learn to promote and refine the energy that truly defines who we are in this life. I further explained that while having a proper perspective of our bodies, feelings and thoughts and harmonizing these aspects was a wonderful beginning, the journey towards a deeper awakening to our true nature starts with recognizing that, as I put it back then, "Everything is energy and so are you."

In my opinion, if this awakening to one's life energy happens not just intellectually, but rather on the being level of the person, then it is what the Japanese word *satori* (悟り), and the Chinese word *wu* (悟) is referencing. In the Zen Buddhist tradition, satori refers to the experience of kenshō, "seeing into one's true nature." Satori and kenshō are commonly translated as enlightenment, a word that is also used to translate bodhi, prajna and Buddhahood. In some circles, "awakening" and "enlightenment" have been imagined as supremely elevated states of existence that most people will never experience. Some even imagine that such a state must mean that one will soon be exiting the body permanently. However, we should recall that when Gautama Siddhartha awoke beneath the bodhi tree and became the Buddha, he continued to live and teach for many more years.

Others believe that such a state is reserved for divinely chosen individuals and is not possible for most of us. But in the Christian verse John 14:12, it is written that Christ said (in this contemporary English version), "I tell you for certain that if you have faith in me, you will do the same things I am doing. You will do even greater things, now that I am going back to the Father."

Let me clarify here that I do not conflate the state of consciousness I describe as "enlightenment" as being the same as that belonging to those who are deemed "Manifestations of God" in the teachings of the Bahá'í Faith, which identifies nine including the Buddha and Jesus Christ.

While the distance between them may be great, the promise of all religions, it seems to me, is that human beings can through their diligence, effort, and sincerity, approach the heights illumined for us by the Manifestations of God. Indeed, the main purpose of my previous book was precisely to provide a non-religious step-by-step guide to how this might be achieved. The main focus of that book was to show how fear stops us from trying new things, from seeing the world in new ways, and God forbid, from questioning what we were taught as children.

In this book, I will turn towards how the beliefs we pick up from the world around us can stop us from growing beyond them. The lessons we learn from parents and teachers shape our understanding of the natural world and our interactions with other people. These lessons can help or hinder our evolution and growth towards our full potential. It is vital we learn to test these lessons learned as children as we get older.

While I have a personal background of growing up in Hong Kong under traditional Chinese culture, it was moving to Los Angeles and experiencing the rapidly changing social landscape of America in the post-Nixon era that informs much who I am today. Reflecting on lessons I have gleaned from the Bahá'í teachings, Jungian psychology, and quantum physics, I will offer one way of understanding the state of the world as it stands today, and how we can thrive here without losing sight of the bigger picture of WHY we are we. I will show how a runaway belief in materialism has devastated the natural world, forced individuals into lives of desperation regardless of their income level and blinded our political and scientific leaders into ignoring the intangible aspects of life leading to a grossly imbalanced society.

In *Physical to Metaphysical*, I touched upon how shortly after I had the experience of "awakening" to the fact that everything is energy and so am I, I learned about books by Robert Monroe, a pioneer of modern consciousness research. In his famous trilogy on "Out of Body" experiences (OBEs), Bob described how while working on sleep learning through audio technology, he discovered binaural sounds (directing a different frequency to each ear via headphones) could stimulate the formation of any desired frequencies in the brain. An unexpected effect of these experiments that he conducted on himself was Bob began having spontaneous OBEs. Reluctantly at first, but soon enthusiastically, Bob delved into these experiences. One of the conclusions he came to after decades of experimentation is death is not the end, and growth that you make to your personality and character will persist and continue on in another life.

While intrigued, I never attempted to have an OBE myself until after I had absorbed some of the teachings of Tom Campbell, a noted physicist and a much younger collaborator of Bob Monroe. Tom's trilogy on the subject, "My Big T.O.E. (theory of everything)," is written for the left-brain, logic-dominant mindset holders to help them approach a very right-brain, intuitive subject. Tom's work helped me understand that much of what we see and feel in an OBE cannot be literally real and can only ever be a metaphor that you must interpret. In fact, physical material reality is also not "literally" real, but rather a personalized sensory data stream that we must interpret.

Or as Einstein explained, "Reality is merely an illusion, albeit a very persistent one…"

Tom's research has allowed me to grasp that what is important in having OBEs is the internal reaction one has to what is experienced. The key is not is it "real?" Rather, it is what did I learn. For me, the very nature of an OBE is that it is perceived as a very real experience that is not like a lucid dream, not like a hallucination, and sometimes as real as waking life.

Later in the book, I will detail how I also began to have OBEs and write about some of them and how they related to events in my physical life. For now, let me just state this: my wife and I have been having such experiences for several years now. At one point, we did try to test if things we see while "out" could be verified later as real and we did so. But soon, I became mainly interested in having more archetypal experiences. In the beginning, it was our own intentions that drove the experiences, but as time went on, we began to have more "directed" situations that seemed geared to teaching certain lessons. In fact, for a period of several months, most of my OBEs were of attending some kind of class.

In the first book, I wrote, "Humanity started our path to global domination by smashing flint stones together to make tools. Now we are smashing atoms together in our search to find the penultimate elemental particle in order to make better tools. In other words, we are collectively still doing the same thing in the same way." In many other ways, we are still doing things the same way as before. While on the surface, technical advances have led to great strides in comfort and convenience for some, social inequality, corruption, manipulation, oppression, and many other problems that have pestered humanity for ages are still festering beneath a sea of apathy and indifference.

And the scale of our social and environmental problems has increased tremendously within just the last century. Our home planet used to be a rather humble place just a hundred years ago. The planes were flimsy and there was no such thing as a computer to speak of. The world has now marked the 100th anniversary of the end of World War I, "the war to end all wars," when a hastily crafted armistice was signed in France on "the eleventh hour of the eleventh day of the eleventh month." World War I was not an end to war, but rather the beginning of endless wars.

Human societies have waged war from the beginning of recorded history and most likely much earlier than that. But the technology of warfare remained the same for centuries until the age of cold steel was replaced by the age of hot lead. But even after the rapid spread of shooting weapons that use gunpowder, it was not until the 1850s that the pace of change began to pick up speed, and by WWI, the means to massacre men had come to what many thought was an acme of destructive power. It was merely the tip of the iceberg...

One hundred years later, the various nuclear powers have conducted more than 2,000 nuclear test explosions. The United States alone is responsible for 1,054 tests by official count of which 219 were atmospheric tests. With India, Pakistan, and North Korea, the world now has eight declared nuclear states, and Israel is widely recognized as having a sizable nuclear arsenal.

Humanity has probed the heavens. We've landed men on the moon and returned them safely. Yet we still suffer from the mental illness of valuing scarcity. Governments regularly destroy massive amounts of food stuff in what they call "price support" action. Diamonds are hoarded to create an illusion of rarity. Useless physical items are collected at jaw-dropping prices due to their uniqueness. Meanwhile, many more unique living beings are allowed to wilt and die from lack of attention or are actively destroyed to make way for "development."

Despite the overthrow of the rule of kings and monarchs, the value system of humanity is currently still mired in a neofeudalistic worship of wealth, status and power. The reason that the seemingly unsolvable social issues caused by our collective behavior persists year after year is that we still do what we are used to doing. Only when human beings change internally will we see change in our external conditions.

While it is possible (if cruel and disingenuous) to blame the victim for social issues like homelessness, ecological issues are now coming to a crisis point as well, and for that we have only our collective selves to blame. The problems with environmental degradation, over-population, pollution, nuclear waste and mass extinction are well-known. Yet, humanity's direction is not changing. When just a year after the Fukushima nuclear disaster, Japan elected a conservative government that doubled down on its nuclear power industry, I was quite depressed. I began to wonder at the state of our world where choices are made that clearly favor a tiny elite while placing tragic burdens on the vast majority.

I understand deeply that many of the elites see the world as quite "fair," and they live with little remorse. "People are dying from all kinds of things," they tell themselves. Everyone has their place and they are just doing what anyone would do if they were in the same place. If you see a chance to "make a kill," you do it, or someone else will. If you see an unfair advantage, you have to take it. In fact, you have to "do it to them before they do it to you!" Under this mindset, you can never have enough or ever drop your guard because everyone is just like you, always looking for a chance to take from the unwitting. Whatever the issue, what's good for you is what is good. Or as the old saying goes, "Where you stand depends on where you sit."

Our humble home planet may be a little crowded and garbage strewn, but it is still easily the nicest on the block. In fact, according to one astrophysicist who came up with a calculation for valuing planets, Earth is worth a bank-breaking $5 quadrillion dollars, unsurprisingly the priciest in the solar system. The admittedly less-than-scientific calculation accounts for such factors as a planet's size, mass, temperature, age, etc. to arrive at a price. Thought up by the solar-system's first planetary appraiser, Greg Laughlin, assistant astronomy and astrophysics professor from the University of California, Santa Cruz, the special formula for determining how much worlds are worth has a subsection on whether or not our cosmic abode retains its value. If we, the human holders of the main lease, fail to see the we are just one part of the biosphere where the real value of the planet resides, fail to live in wholeness with all of the life forms of the planet, and make the place unlivable, it won't be worth a penny.

Unfortunately, under the Trump administration, division and conflict, not wholeness and unity are the themes. But for some time before the rise of Trump, environmentalism has been on the decline. Public polling and election results indicate that the number of people who see the value of living in wholeness with nature have been declining in the United States. Understandably, if someone is raised to see a world of competition, they are not going to see the "value" of something as vague as "wholeness." Furthermore, for them, nature is NOT wholeness, it is a war of all against all, eat or be eaten, the survival of the strong. After all, they would say, in a struggle for survival, even a vegetable knows that you need to fight for your place in the sun.

Chapter One

A PLACE IN THE SUN

Human drama has a timeless quality about it. We read the tragedies from ancient Greece with familiarity and recognition. Shakespeare translates well into modern times and his plays have been retold variously as a gangster movie and a space opera, among others. Most of that drama is prescribed by birth and death, wanting and getting, betrayal and vengeance. But occasionally, one of the characters can see a little further than that. This book is about moving past just being concerned with finding your place in the sun and prospering, or getting back at whoever took your spot.

From its humble origins, life on this planet has come a long way. As small one-celled creatures evolved into various forms and learned to use resources and habitats, both competition and cooperation was needed to move the process forward. Eventually, humanity emerged and became one among many bipedal apes.

Acknowledged history and mainstream archaeology will tell you that we became the dominant species on this planet rather suddenly on an evolutionary timeline. Culture seemed to spring up according to a set script in ancient Mesopotamia with sophisticated concepts of astronomy, mathematics and warfare emerging as if from a blank slate. Soon, we became the biggest influence on the environment, altering entire regions of the planet, mainly by making them into deserts.

With modern technology, we are remaking the face of the land and bridging the vast oceans. Even the poles are alive with high tech activities or all kinds. Society is becoming increasingly centralized. Small farms are disappearing and agriculture is dominated by giant corporations. Farming practices have become so removed from their natural source that most grains are now produced from neutered GMO seeds created for their ability to resist pesticides. Industrial meat production hides the way animals are packed together and how they suffer. Chemicals are overused to keep them alive and make them gain weight. As a result of long-term consumption of the products from these "ranches", people are stricken with all kinds of chronic ailments not known to earlier generations.

By its very nature, cruelty to the animals is a part of the meat-making process. But often, it blossoms into disgusting examples of our inhumanity towards the creatures we eat. Male chicks not needed for reproduction are ground up alive by egg producers. Workers are repeatedly filmed by whistle blowers abusing animals in outrageous ways. Animals are sometimes injected with tap water while alive to increasing their weight in an illegal, but probably all too common, practice.

While most people who eat meat produce this way remain blithely unaware of the suffering we are causing to the animals before they are killed, the effect of industrialized meat production is all around us. Ask people where they would rank meat-eating as an issue of concern to the general public, and most might be surprised to hear you suggest that it is an issue at all. To eat meat or not (or how much) is a private matter, they might say. Maybe it has some implications for your heart, especially if you are overweight. But it's not one of the high-profile public issues you'd expect presidential candidates to debate. Certainly it's not up there with terrorism, the economy, the (current) war, or "the environment..."

However, the astute few recognize our voracious desire for meat-eating is having a wide range of environmental impact. These implications may seem relatively small taken separately. Here, some reports of tropical rainforests being cut down to accommodate cattle ranchers. There, more reports of native grasslands being destroyed by grazing. Recently, environmentalists are beginning to grasp that meat-eating belongs on the same scale of importance as the kinds of issues that have energized Amazon Watch, or Conservation International, or Greenpeace.

As environmental science is applied to understand the issue, it becomes apparent that human appetite for animal flesh is a driving force behind virtually every major category of environmental damage now threatening our future: deforestation, erosion, fresh water scarcity, air and water pollution, climate change, loss of biodiversity...

To produce meat is also extremely energy-demanding. The burning of fossil fuels for energy and animal agriculture are two of the biggest contributors to global warming, along with deforestation. According to the World Resources Institute of the UN Food and Agriculture Organization, fossil fuel-based energy is responsible for about 60% of human greenhouse gas emissions, with deforestation at about 18%, and animal agriculture around 16%.

Less apparent then the environmental impact of meat consumption is the contributing role it plays in continuing social injustice, destabilization of communities, spread of disease in poorer areas with no reliable refrigeration, and the problem with "bush meat." Even more subtle, but nonetheless real, is the psychological effect of taking animal flesh into one's body. If it is reasonable to believe that physical illness can be caused by long-term consumption of meat laden with chemicals and pharmaceuticals, is it not just as reasonable (and intuitively you already know it) to consider that you can be made emotionally sick by absorbing the hormones and other secretions brought on by the terror and suffering experienced by that flesh? This linkage is made all the worse by the industrial practice to not drain the blood of the animals during slaughtering, keeping the blood in the packaged meat so as to increase the overall weight.

Many religions have proscribed the eating of meat or certain types of meat. In the Bahá'í faith, vegetarianism is encouraged but not required. However, the Bahá'í writings ask us, as human beings, to show kindness to all creatures, especially animals. So, when one considers what happens to animals "produced" in our farm factories, raised in overcrowded and unhealthy conditions from birth only to end their lives in horrific slaughterhouses, it gives one pause. Perhaps that is why meat is sold in neatly packed pieces so we don't have to think about the living creature that died under terrible conditions to make it available.

When I reflect on this issue, I always remember these words from Abdu'l-Baha:

"...man is not in need of meat, nor is he obliged to eat it. Even without eating meat he would live with the utmost vigour and energy. ...Truly, the killing of animals and the eating of their meat is somewhat contrary to pity and compassion, and if one can content oneself with cereals, fruit, oil and nuts... it would undoubtedly be better and more pleasing."

My parents were both cooks and meat was something we grew up relishing. In Cantonese culinary culture, eating anything that moves is a long-established tradition, and I must confess to having eaten some pretty "exotic" animals. However, without exception, I did not enjoy these special meals and only took part as a social obligation. A part of these dinners is the showing of the live animal before they slaughter it (so you can see what you are getting), and that always put a damper on things for me. Since the writing of *Physical to Metaphysical*, my wife and I have made a determined move to a vegetarian diet. We started it as an experiment, and the experiment was a success! Stopping eating meat did make us feel "better and more pleasing."

When I was little, my mom had a friend who believed that eating a lot of meat meant she was "well off." Most of her meals had to feature several meat dishes, and when she had guests, vegetarians were not invited. She died of her diet a few years after my mom last heard from her. The immediate cause was heart attack, but the real cause was all that meat.

I think Albert Einstein sums it up best when he said:

"Nothing will benefit human health and increase chances of survival of life on Earth as much as the evolution to a vegetarian diet."

And perhaps nothing has decreased the chances of the survival of life on Earth as the arrival of nuclear weapons. Psychologically, obtaining the "power of the atom" was a cause for massive ego inflation in human beings. "Now I am become death, the destroyer of worlds," remarked theoretical physicist J. Robert Oppenheimer, widely credited as the "father of the atomic bomb," right after the first atomic explosion. Hardly... that first test blast barely destroyed a mile of desert sand, but Oppenheimer did correctly predict that, collectively, humanity would soon stockpile more than enough atomic bombs to destroy several worlds.

Against all reason, just the two superpowers during the Cold War amassed more nuclear weapons than needed to destroy the entire land mass of the planet an estimated 45 times over. With the success of the world's first agreements to actually reduce nuclear arms, known as SALT I and SALT II (signed by the United States and the USSR in 1972 and 1979, respectively), the world stepped back from the brink of annihilation. The problem soon became proliferation of nuclear capable missiles and warheads to "rogue nations."

The "good news" is that the United States, Russia, China and the world's other nuclear-armed countries now possess enough fissile material to blow up the planet "only" about five times over. In 2010, the Pentagon revealed it was at that time the proud owner of 5,113 made-in-the USA nuclear warheads. That's down from a high of more than 31,000 in the late 1960s. These weapons of mass destruction are still thought of as the pinnacle of military might and in the current world situation they represent the ultimate guarantor of a nation-state's "place in the sun" in the international community. It is this reasoning that drove India, Pakistan, and North Korea to take the plunge. But if diplomacy fails, and conventional war leads to nuclear war, we will truly become the destroyer of our own world. The greatest present danger is the standoff between nuclear-armed India and Pakistan. Behind this physical confrontation is the psychic struggle between two religious-based belief systems.

The greatest danger in a nuclear war is that even one in which only a fraction of the available weapons are used, the end result will be enough to collapse the fragile natural systems of the planet, already under siege from centuries of industrial pollution. We could see a "feather that broke the camel's back" moment even with a "limited" nuclear exchange. The chance of such a "limited nuclear war" is much higher now than during the height of the Cold War due to the fading away of the Mutually Assured Destruction (MAD) doctrine.

The balance of terror between the US and USSR during the Cold War prevented direct combat between NATO and the Warsaw Pact countries, but even under the constraining threat of nuclear escalation, the fight for "national security" was unrelenting. After the collapse of the Soviet Union, initial international optimism turned to dread as fear was drummed up by the Bush administration that Iraq had weapons of mass destruction and nuclear ambitions. In hindsight, it is easy to see it was propaganda, and badly done propaganda at that.

President Trump began talking up the North Korean threat early in his presidential campaign and since his election has repeatedly sent the military into the area to threaten its regime. Trump claims that his aggressive tactics were the reason Kim Jung Un agreed to a bilateral summit without conditions. In reality, holding a bilateral summit without preconditions is little more than giving North Korea international cover to continue expanding its nuclear program unchecked. Following the summit, there was some discussion of a deal to denuclearize the whole Korean peninsula. However, whatever talk there is of cobbling a deal together that could put North Korea's nuclear genie back into the bottle, in my opinion it is too late for that. While the immediate problem with North Korea is kicked down the road, Trump has thrown the internationally brokered nuclear deal with Iran into doubt, and Iran is being pressured once again to open its nuclear program to outside inspection. Iran has replied to the move by the Trump administration with threats that it will redouble its previous efforts if it is attacked with "unwarranted" sanctions. Meanwhile, Israel is threatening to attack Iran if it continues to move towards nuclear capability… The world is in more danger of "limited" nuclear warfare at this moment than ever.

Far from the dizzying heights of international affairs where nations struggle for their share of the limelight, for the average person on the street, "a place in the sun" just means getting a good job, fighting for a promotion, buying what you want, winning social recognition, and marrying "a good catch." This was certainly the worldview transmitted to me by my parents and peers. As I got older and started working, I aimed to acquire the lifestyle of the middle-class American. However, through the experiences described in *Physical to Metaphysical*, my life course became rather unconventional. And I steered that course with unconventional choices. On the surface, it was remarkable that I quit a lucrative and prestigious job just as I was about to enter the senior ranks, to care for my widowed mother. On a deeper level, I was already seeking some form of liberation from the life that I no longer felt a part of.

That choice gave me the freedom to complete my doctorate and led me to reconnect with the person I would marry a few years later. After we were married in 2010, my wife and I worked through a number of relationship issues and helped each other grow past our family histories. In hindsight, I can see that being in a loving relationship definitely sped up our personal growth. Having established a materially and emotionally nurturing situation, we began to seek for... more. Not more of the same, but categorically more. After some effort in this direction, I experienced what I perceived as an "enlightenment" moment.

As detailed in the first book, that moment came after years of preparation and occurred around the same time I formulated the "Inner Sun" technique of meditation. As I fully internalized the lesson that I did not need the world to give me my "place in the sun," my reluctance to personally explore the psychic spaces described by Bob Monroe and Tom Campbell melted away. As I wrote in *Physical to Metaphysical*, "I had wanted to try going 'out of body' ever since reading about it in Bob Monroe's books, but residual fear kept me from going for it." Eventually I felt I had to try it for myself, and in August of 2015, I told my wife I would try to do it. She was a bit cautious, believing that OBEs were just variations of the more lucid dream-like experiences that she was familiar with. Not knowing what to expect despite Bob's books, Tom's videos, and many other sources I have studied, I finally just went for it.

However, the full story is that our out-f-body adventures were kicked off by my wife having what I can only term a "close encounter of the three-and-a-half kind."

Let me elaborate:

The use of kinds of "Close Encounters" to rate UFO experiences was started by astronomer J. Allen Hynek during his work with the Air Force's Project Blue Book, and laid out in his 1972 book, *The UFO Experience: A Scientific Inquiry*. He introduced the first three kinds of encounters, and more sub-types of close encounters were later added by others, but these additional categories are not universally accepted by UFO researchers, mainly because they depart from the scientific rigor that Hynek aimed to bring to ufology.

In Hynek's scale, a Close Encounter of the First kind consists of visual sightings of an unidentified flying object seemingly less than 500 feet away that show an appreciable angular extension and considerable detail. A Close Encounters of the Second kind is an UFO event in which a physical effect is alleged. This can be interference in the functioning of a vehicle or electronic device, animals reacting or a physiological effect such as paralysis or heat and discomfort in the witness. Physical trace like impressions in the ground, scorched or otherwise affected vegetation, or a chemical trace would also qualify.

Close Encounters of the Third kind, which was adopted as the title of the famous Steven Spielberg movie, is one where the encounter includes an animated creature being present. These can include humanoids, robots, and humans who seem to be occupants or pilots of a UFO. A fourth kind was added after the "abduction" phenomenon began to be widely reported.

I will detail my wife's UFO experience as well as my own, and how I used OBEs to find out more about them in chapter three. In hindsight, I can clearly see that it was my inability to find a satisfactory explanation for these kinds of "encounters" (mine occurred years before I met my wife) that ultimately pushed me to try to find answers by using out-of-body travel. My very first attempt at going out of body was kicked off by this intention. And it was successful. The result of that first experience did succeed in at least partially answering one question I had about the beings that I took to be extraterrestrials of some kind – where do they live? Apparently somewhere underground.

It was very exciting to succeed on the first try, but when I tried the second time, I found I was unable for some reason to return to the same "place." Soon the experiences became less grounded in my intent and more guided in nature. After I began to experience a series of religious-themed journeys that helped me to consolidate and confirm my faith, I found myself settling into a series of experiences that involved going to a kind of school, culminating in a very strange and unique OBE that I did not initiate, but rather perceived as being pulled out of sleep and into giving a lecture. I must confess that after a short time, I got bored with going to classes while out of body. Thankfully, I eventually "graduated" to more interesting experiences and deeper lessons.

After the months of "class," I become successful at having controlled OBEs regularly and was mostly able to direct them by my own intention. Around that time, I read that TEPCO, the Japanese company responsible for cleaning up Fukushima, had lost track of (translation: dumped in the sea) untold tons of highly radioactive waste water, and also had no idea where the melted clump of core material had fallen to. Well, I was quite depressed by this news, and while in this state of depression and worry at the state of the planet, I began to have a series of OBEs that helped me understand why things are the way they are....

Out-of-Body Experiences from November 2015

By this point, the thrill of successfully doing out-of-body travel had worn off. Many times, the experience would just peter out as I lost focus or because I lacked a clear intention, and I would just end up in a haze or fall asleep. On this particular night, I went through the "classic" phases of coming out of my physical body, seeing the room, then flying away to some destination.

I feel the need to reiterate here, that while some might surmise that OBEs are just a sort of dream, albeit a very lucid one, I must stress that for me there is an absolute degree of difference between the lucid dreaming which I have experienced and out-of-body travel. Bear in mind these are intimately personal experiences in nature and while hard to describe in words the exactitude of the difference, I have a distinct memory of feeling and saying to myself, "this is different."

Like the religious themed OBEs I had, this series felt initiated and guided by an external intent...

One night while out of body and just wandering around, a glowing piece of paper fell into my hands. On it was written, *"Find 1850."* I looked around and there was no one. A powerful sense of curiosity lingered with me after I woke up. Was it the year? No, somehow I knew it was a place.

Over the next several weeks I kept trying to see if it might be a hotel room, a locker number, or even a flight number, I finally focused on finding 1850 as a house number, but I could never see any place with that exact number.

Finally, one night, on the verge of giving up, I had a breakthrough...

I feel gently drawn out of body and immediately find myself looking at a very large mansion sitting on a slight rise. Upon closer inspection I could see in gold lettering the address reads 1850 C. The mansion is surrounded by a high fence with no visible gate. I see a small sign that reads, "service entrance." Excitedly I walked to the side and am a little surprised that hidden a little behind the large mansion is a dilapidated-looking warehouse with sheet metal walls and a rusty door. I approach the door and push it open. It is very dark, but I enter anyway. Immediately upon entering, a young-looking woman with dirt on her face and tattered clothes walks up to me and tries to put a bag over my head. I push her off and inspect her face. She seems drugged or mentally impaired. I ask her what is this place, but she doesn't answer and just keeps trying to put the bag over my head. After a bit of shoving, she gives up and walks off. I take the chance to look around in the dim light... I make out stacks of cages about five feet square all around me. Inside each cage is a person!

As my vision adjusts to the dimness, I am aghast. Some in the cages have tattered clothes, some are naked. Many cower with bags still over their heads. I get the impression of an immense human slaughterhouse. Thankfully I do not see actual killing or blood around, but the feeling that these captives are just waiting to die is overwhelming. I notice that all have chains resting on some part of their body, but none are shackled and the cages are not locked. Disgusted and appalled at what I am seeing, I have no time to form more of a reaction, as suddenly the woman reappears with an Asian-looking man in a suit.

"Put the bag on and get in the cage," he says impatiently. I shake my head. He starts to scream and shake his fist at me, then he makes some kind of gesture and from the darkness above us a giant policeman starts to descend slowly. I notice the cop is white and looks to be about twelve feet tall.

"Hit him," the Asian man orders, and the cop starts to pull out his baton.

Already very emotional from the scene, I become outraged, "You have no right to hit me! I demand justice!"

The cop looks uncertain and hesitates. I continue to yell and holler. After a bit of this, I say, "you can hit me, but first you have to tell me why?"

At this point, he looks at me and then looks at the other man who says nothing. As he turns back to me, he slowly shrinks down in size.

"I have to ask the management," the cop says, now normal-sized. The two men turn away and they both levitate into the dark. As they fade into the space above, the woman walks away and I am left alone in the warehouse with the cages that recede into seemingly endless dark.

After a brief moment, a light appears above me, and an echoing voice says, "You are in the wrong place, you may go." The door opens and as I walk out I see the people in the cages turn away from the light coming in. Once outside, I feel overwhelmed with a sense of release and relief. I walk down to a nearby beach and wash my feet in the water. There are colorful fish swimming in small schools and the sunlight glittering off the waves look like clusters of jewels are showering into the air. I am filled with a wondrous emotion that I can't put into words...

Over the next week or so of reflecting on the experience, I came to realize that multiple sets of symbolism could be detected. The mansion represented the reality of the privileged elites of the world and it is linked and sustained in many ways by the human warehouse, which represented the world of those trapped in poverty and despair, hidden next to it. The bureaucrat and the policeman enforce the system and don't ask why. The cages are real enough, but they are not locked. No one is "destined" to be poor. You have to let them put the bag over your head, and the chains you put on yourself. Despair is the bag and hopelessness is the chain. However, even if this terrible scene is in some ways representative of the state of the world today, it is possible to not make yourself a part of it, and then there is a door for you.

A few months later, I was reading some financial news and it mentioned that the Federal Reserve Headquarters is actually several buildings in Washington, DC, and while most people think of the Board of Governors building on Constitution Ave. as "the Federal Reserve" (as I had until reading said article), the actual work of "running the financial system" was done at the building at 1850 K Street.

Let me close this portion with this quote from Henry Ford, founder of the Ford Motor Company. "It is well enough that people of the nation do not understand our banking and monetary system, for if they did, I believe there would be a revolution before tomorrow morning."

Who is the winner, who is the loser?

From a materialistic perspective, it is clear who the winners and losers are in the "game of life." There actually was a board game called "The Game of Life" when I was kid. And the way to win was to get a good job, make money, and buy more stuff than the other players. Using a physical scale to reckon things, it would seem it is true that, "the one who dies with the most toys wins!" Don't the photos the fabulously rich post online show how happy they are partying with celebrities on their yachts? Don't you feel inadequate or at least envious that you are not in a position to post similar pictures? Having known personally a number of people who are wealthy enough to live the "lifestyle of the rich and famous," I could not help but see that they always seemed to be trying very hard to show everyone around them, most importantly themselves, how "happy and rich" they were by having to "top" their "friends" by doing more and more expensive things.

In China, I had a number of consultations with newly affluent people who came to see me precisely because they had obtained the material success that they had been working to get, and now they are surprised that emotionally they are still in the same place as before. Why aren't they as happy as they expected they would be? In fact, often they are even more unhappy and frustrated then when they were struggling to "make it." Some bury this feeling with just making more and more money, working harder and longer for some material sign post of "I made it."

For most people, the travails of this newly affluent class are a luxury they can't imagine. The financially squeezed middle-class is programmed to emulate the tastes of the affluent, but they simply can't keep up. Longer and longer work hours have led to some people dropping dead from the pressure. In Japan, karōshi (過労死), which can be translated literally as overwork death, has been known for decades. It is now publicly accepted that for Japanese people, this kind of "occupational hazard" (sudden mortality!) is just a part of modern life. The major medical causes of karōshi deaths are heart attack and stroke due to stress and a bad diet. This phenomenon is also widespread in South Korea, where it is referred to as gwarosa (과로사). In China, overwork-induced death is becoming more common, but less recognized (guo lao si 过劳死). I am sure the issue is also present in other highly industrialized societies, and just has not been widely discussed.

The pressure to work relentlessly is stronger on higher-paid workers rather than on unskilled labor due to both the lure of reward and the fear of being left behind. Someone in a position with things to gain and much to lose is easier to hoodwink into judging their worth purely on a material basis. It is not as easy to fool someone into wrecking their health when they don't see much to gain beyond their limited pay. However, if they are desperate to pay bills and have overdue debts...

Outside of the rapidly growing economies of East Asia, the more common malady is unemployment, indebtedness, and declining incomes. In the United States, the opioid epidemic is a symptom of the emotional fallout from people who are unable to obtain the material situation they crave, but know of no other way to seek satisfaction. According to the US Drug Enforcement Administration, nearly half of all opioid overdose deaths in 2016 involved prescription opioids. Starting in 1999, overdose death rates, sales, and substance abuse treatment admissions related to opioid pain relievers all increased substantially. By 2015, annual overdose deaths from heroin alone surpassed deaths from both car accidents and guns, with other opioid overdose deaths also on the rise.

Despite the increased use of painkillers, there has been no change in the amount of pain reported in the US This has led to differing medical opinions, with some researchers noting that there is little evidence that opioids are effective for chronic pain not caused by cancer. Nonetheless with approximately 4.4 percent of the world population, the United States annually consumes about **80 percent** of the global pharmaceutical opioid supply.

So the picture seems to be that the skilled worker in a rising economy works himself to death because he is afraid of falling down to the lower rungs of the economic ladder, and the unskilled worker in a slowing economy drugs himself to death because he is already there. Seems like there are no winners for those who find themselves in the "working class" as the world passes the 2020 mark...

Most working people don't think about the "big picture." They see life as enough of a struggle to earn the money you need, insure against all the pitfalls out there, and still make time to deal with family and other people to ever give much thought to the nature of the universe or any greater purpose to "being here." If money is tight, the pressure to just "make it" can take all one's attention. This is the "financial cage" that you can find yourself in with a few bad decisions early in life or just a bit of bad luck. But even if things go well, it is easy to be blinded by only seeing the "newest" toy you must have! This is the "bag" you put over your own head. The very practical and logical highest value for this materialistic mindset is "Live long and prosper." Unfortunately, in a competitive, neo-feudal system, live long and prosper for some has meant exploited and made dependent for most.

The "facilitator" class in such systems lives a precarious existence and suffers from envy of the "owner" class and dread of becoming a part of the "resource" class. It is noteworthy that corporate culture has replaced the term "personnel" with the more revealing term "human resource." The dictionary definition of "Resource": a source of supply, support, or aid, especially one that can be readily drawn down when needed. I personally find calling a living human being a resource to be rather offensive. When I left the State Department, they still had Personnel Officers, its HR now...

Members of the "facilitator" class sometimes actually understand the system better than some born to the "owner" class. When the more self-aware are confronted by moral dilemmas and tugs of conscience, they tell themselves the "system" is the way it is for a good reason. The "bosses" are where they are because they are smarter. The "owners" of the economy are not always smarter, but they are always much more informed and powerful in a material sense than the average person.

The "wolves of Wall Street" type proudly proclaimed they were the "Masters of the Universe" during the long bull run before the 2008 "Big Short" moment. But they can't forget that they are just on the higher echelons of the "facilitator" class responsible for fleecing the "human resource." The thrust of my argument is of course that we can NEVER judge the winner and loser from a material point of view, because we are NOT just material beings. Winners follow their consciences.

Remember Greg Smith, the former Goldman Sachs employee who infamously quit Wall Street via a *New York Times* article? Smith revealed that the investment bank routinely took advantage of charities and pension funds in order to increase its profits. In his CBS News' 60 Minutes interview, he told how traders laughingly referred to unsophisticated clients as "muppets." Taking money from these clients was the top goal of the bank's salespeople because they would take the highest risk and pay the most fees. His frustration with that culture was such that he "literally wanted to hit the board of directors over the head." Sadly, Smith is rather unique and nothing was done as a result of his revelations and the big banks have continued on about the same.

The scale of the fraud in the banking industry was further revealed in the Wells Fargo account fraud scandal. Much outrage was brought about by the creation of millions of fraudulent savings and checking accounts on behalf of Wells Fargo clients without their consent, and the subsequent charging of fees for unwanted products. The scandal was made worse when it was shown that management had fired employees who complained about the practice. Various regulatory bodies, including the Consumer Financial Protection Bureau, fined the company hundreds of millions of dollars as a result of the illegal activity, and the company faces additional civil and criminal suits.

Wells Fargo clients began to notice the fraud after being charged unanticipated fees and receiving unexpected credit or debit cards or lines of credit. Initial reports blamed individual Wells Fargo branch workers and managers for the problem, as well as sales incentives associated with selling multiple "solutions" or financial products. The real responsibility was later found to rest with pressure from higher-level management to open as many accounts as possible through cross-selling.

As the economic contradictions first revealed in the "Great Recession" that began in 2008 continue to accelerate as a result of the Federal Reserve's decision to cover up the reality of the situation, the pressure on the public is sure to build. Using the "economic emergency" caused by the shutdowns to combat the coronavirus outbreak as cover, the Federal Reserve literally announced QE (quantitative easing AKA money from nothing) "to infinity." The danger of too much easy money for the economy is not unknown. Richard W. Fisher, the former President and CEO of the Federal Reserve Bank of Dallas, (retired in 2015) was one of the few people at the Fed who admitted the policy of "endless printing" was going to turn out badly.

As US equity markets began to unravel immediately after then Fed Chair Janet Yellen began hiking interest rates, Fisher belatedly came out on CNBC decrying the Federal Open Market Committee's decision to launch a third round of QE, saying that he "voted against doing QE3" and that QE3 was "one step too far." Fisher went as far as to say the "front-loading" of so much easy credit to create what he called a "wealth effect" of rising stock prices was like putting the economy on "financial cocaine and heroin."

Yellen's seeming willingness to change direction from flirting with negative interest rates (don't laugh, there are real bonds that people literally pay to hold) to a tiny rate increase scared investors addicted to easy money. Fortunately for these "addicts," the action has moved from monetary policy to fiscal policy. What is the difference between fiscal and monetary policy? Monetary policy is implemented by a central bank mainly through setting interest rates, while fiscal policy decisions on Federal spending are set by the national government. However, both monetary and fiscal policy may be used to influence the performance of the economy in the short run. The "wealth effect" is now the Trump administration's willingness to borrow more and more money from the Fed to spend on defense and his Mexican Wall. With the Corona outbreak, both political parties are now intent on unleashing a tidal wave of deficit spending to "rescue" America.

But there is little doubt the ultimate financial losers will again be present and future American taxpayers. With the federal government's annual budget deficit set to widen significantly in the next few years, and expected to top $1 trillion in 2020 (much more with projected spending for bailouts and stimulus packages), the total national debt, which has exceeded $21 trillion, will soar to unimaginable heights. According to the Congressional Budget Office, by 2028, debt held by the public will almost match the size of the nation's economy, reaching 96 percent of GDP, the highest level since the end of World War II and well past the level where without constant central bank manipulation and money printing, interest rates would have risen much higher. When interests rates inevitably go up, higher borrowing costs for the private sector will reveal that behind the massive amounts of stock buybacks used by big company CEOs to reduce the number of outstanding shares in order to show a higher per share value (it's how bonuses are calculated), most of them are losing money, and have been for years.

Who is going to win and who is going to lose as this unfolds? Beyond the maintenance of your household, how much money is really required? Is focusing on money unproductive to one's inner development? Each of us will have to find our own answers to these questions, however, someone who works to the point of even harming his health, from the light of an inner need, even if he were to die before he completes his self-appointed task, probably perceives his journey as pleasant, as he did what he chose for himself. Another, who possesses few material comforts, has no outer ambition, and always seems to be introspective, has no need for emotional anesthetics if he is the ruler of his inner world.

Perhaps the "real winners" are the people who are born into the "owner" class, who never have to worry about money or work for a living? People lucky enough to have their whole life laid out in front of them like that must be guaranteed a place in heaven, right?

Personal Interlude: Stairway to Heaven

When I think of Madame D, this song always comes to mind…

"There's a lady who's sure

All that glitters is gold
And she's buying a stairway to heaven...
When she gets there she knows
If the stores are all closed
With a word she can get what she came for..."

In 1983, I moved to San Francisco for university. Through a family connection, I was introduced to a very wealthy couple to occasionally help out as a server at their fancy dinner parties. I had worked as a waiter in high school so this was not much different, and I welcomed the chance to make some quick cash. I soon learned that the lady of the manor, Madame D, was the real boss. Her current husband, the second one, used to be her stockbroker and married from facilitator into the owner class.

Turns out Madame D had spent several years of her childhood in Shanghai during the city's heyday of Western penetration in the early '30s. Her family was in the shipping business and they lived in a large mansion near the Bund or *Waitan* (外滩, literally: "Outer Beach"), the famous waterfront area in central Shanghai. She had very fond memories of her Chinese ah-mah (nanny) that translated into a life-long preference for Chinese servants.

When I first met her, she was in her late 70s, but still alert and in good health. Having inherited all of the family fortune by outliving her cousins, her personal wealth was measured in the billions of dollars. For whatever reason, she took a shine to me, and offered me the chance to house-sit at the mansion in San Francisco while she and her husband would spend the summer months at one of their many other estates. In this way, I came to know quite a bit about her by way of direct observation, and via her Chinese servants, the insider gossip.

She was quite representative of her segment of the socio-economic pie. Politically, she was a conservative Republican, but not particularly religious. She was definitely a racist under the textbook sense of the word: The belief in the superiority of one race over another resulting in prejudice towards people based on their race or ethnicity. Often she would express with pure sincerity the belief that humans can be subdivided into distinct groups that are different due to innate capacities and social behavior, and that traits and preferences are specific to certain races. Less clearly stated, but implicit was that these races can be ranked as inferior or superior. While homosexuality is not a race, she was sure that gays had "the best artistic people." A glamorous socialite in her younger years, she maintained the limelight through massive donations to the Opera well into her twilight years.

A lifetime of wealth and comfort bred in her a dreadful fear of the world beyond "rich white people land." Although she lived in an area with the lowest crime rate in San Francisco, she built a twelve feet tall wall in front of her mansion. She insisted the servants turn on the alarm and not walk around after dark. After her husband died, she needed to lock her bedroom door to sleep at night.

As recounted by those who spent the most time with her, the live-in servants, the last few years of her life were not something anyone would envy. Madame D would often drink alone and cry over her loneliness. She also couldn't "let anyone see her this way." After falling and breaking her hip, she became bedridden. The last time I saw her alive was to visit her after her fall. She was drugged up and happy, but expressed a readiness to pass on. "Time to bye bye," was the last thing she said to me. Sadly for her, it was not her time, not for many more years...

It turned out her fate was to live ten more years, bedridden and slowly losing touch with reality. Like Howard Hughes, Madame D's final years are a bit of a mystery. Even the live-in servants were not allowed to enter her room unless on order of her doctors. A rotating team of a dozen nurses attended her around the clock, but she still developed bed sores and would often soil herself. It was not clear if she even knew where she was near the end...

Robert Plant, who penned the words for Stairway to Heaven, explained the lyrics were "about a woman getting everything she wanted all the time without giving back any thought or consideration. The first line begins with that cynical sweep of the hand... and it softened up after that."

Your head is humming and it won't go
In case you don't know

The piper's calling you to join him
Dear lady, can you hear the wind blow
And did you know
Your stairway lies on the whispering wind

While I never had a chance to ask about her beliefs concerning what comes after death, I could guess that they would probably be based on the watered-down Christianity she professed at other people's funerals. Perhaps she was expecting nothing at all? But if she was expecting heaven, I am sure her heaven might be very much like her favorite place while on Earth, San Francisco's Union Square shopping district. Or perhaps it's a version of the *Waitan* of her childhood? In any case, it could be only the heaven of a child because she never grew up very much while she was alive.

After I learned I could go "out of body," I would sometimes see what appeared to be departed spirits that lingered in this world. Perhaps influenced by what I read in Bob Monroe's books, I also saw the three types of "dead people" he described. Those who seem to just repeat some favored activity from the prior life, those who seem confused, and those who cause trouble. I also saw instances of people waiting to be reincarnated. I tried to see where Madame D had gone and only caught an impression of a little girl, a single child... Like most Chinese people, her servants were staunch believers in reincarnation, and they were certain that she would come back as a poor person since, in their opinion, she wasn't a good rich person (i.e. more generous to them).

Let me turn now to beliefs concerning life after death. Of all the beliefs we hold, this one is perhaps the most influential on our attitudes, perceptions and behaviors.

Belief in reincarnation appears to have been universal among ancient human societies. The word "reincarnation" derives from Latin, literally meaning, "entering the flesh again." The Greek equivalent metempsychosis derives from meta (change) and empsykhoun (to put a soul into), a term attributed to Pythagoras. An alternate term is transmigration implying migration from life (body) to life. Reincarnation implies that an aspect of every human being (or all living beings in some cultures) continues to exist after death. This aspect can be considered soul or mind or consciousness or something transcendent, but it is always envisioned as immortal.

Death in this view is to be reborn in the form of a human being, or animal, or plant, or spirit, or as a being in some other non-human realm of existence. The "technical" aspect of reincarnation is perhaps most developed in Indian culture. The idea of reincarnation has early roots in the Vedic period (c. 1500 – c. 500 BCE). Hinduism's Rigveda makes references to reincarnation. Though these early textual layers of the Vedas, from the 2nd millennium BCE, mention and anticipate the doctrine of Karma and rebirth, the idea is not yet fully developed. It is in the early Upanishads, which are pre-Buddha and pre-Mahavira (Janism), where these ideas are more explicitly developed with detailed descriptions of the different "bodies" that surround the soul, or Ātman in Sanskrit, a word that probably translates best as innermost self. In the Jaina philosophy, it is taught that the soul (Jiva) exists and is eternal, passing through cycles of transmigration and rebirth.

Although the majority of denominations within the Abrahamic religions of Judaism, Christianity, and Islam do not believe that individuals reincarnate, particular groups within these religions do teach that reincarnation happens; these groups include the mainstream historical and contemporary followers of Kabbalah, the Cathars, the Alawites, the Druze, and the Rosicrucians. Charles Fillmore, the founder of Unity Church, also teaches reincarnation. In the Roman era, reincarnation was characteristic of most of the popular philosophies including Neoplatonism, Orphism, Hermeticism, Manicheanism, and Gnosticism.

The reality of reincarnation was given support by the work of Dr. Ian Stevenson (1918-2007), a psychiatrist at the University of Virginia's School of Medicine for 50 years. He was Chair of the Department of Psychiatry from 1957 to 1967, and founded the University of Virginia's breakthrough Division of Perceptual Studies (DPS). Under Stevenson's directorship, the DPS investigated para-psychological phenomena such as reincarnation, near-death experiences, out-of-body experiences, after-death communications, deathbed visions, altered states of consciousness and instances of psychic abilities. He became internationally recognized for his research into reincarnation by discovering evidence suggesting that memories and physical scars from injuries can be transferred from one lifetime to another. Stevenson traveled extensively over a period of 40 years, investigating 3,000 cases of children around the world who can recall having past lives. His meticulous research presented evidence that such children had unusual abilities, illnesses, phobias and philias which could not be explained by the environment or heredity, but did correlate with causes from their remembered lives.

After my out-of-body experiences showed me what I took as evidence of reincarnation, I realized that I needed to come to terms between what I was perceiving and the teachings of the Bahá'í Faith.

The Bahá'í Faith rejects the notion that reincarnation is required. Instead it offers a far-reaching belief system that presents God's love for humanity as the purpose behind creation. Human beings begin the first stage of our spiritual progress at birth, and as we are enriched with acquisition of virtues and discovery of innate noble qualities in this earthly life, we mature spiritually. After death, this process of spiritual maturation continues throughout the limitless spiritual worlds of God eternally.

The Bahá'í teachings changes the age-old motivation for doing good from hope of heaven and fear of hell, or desire for a reward in the next life under reincarnation, to a continuous and uplifting spiritual progress. The Bahá'í Faith provides a deeper understanding of the spirit and its relationship to the physical body. The body is of the animal kingdom while the human spirit is regarded as God's supreme talisman, and upon death, the spirit leaves behind this world of dust, limitations, weaknesses, and darkness for the next world of freedom, perfection and light. The "birth" of the spirit is seen as analogous to the birth from the limited world of the womb into the vast outside world of colors, sounds, fragrances, tastes and textures.

Thus, there remains no reason for man's spirit to return to this material netherworld and become attached to a plant, animal or even another human body. After its severance from the human body, the human spirit, with its **acquired virtues** (emphasis mine) and God's unique gift of free will, then will soar and journey through the expanse of never-ending spiritual worlds, gaining an ever-greater measure of bounties and grace, and becoming ever worthier of God's companionship.

I completely concur with this view of the nature of creation and that human beings are capable of acquiring the virtues and noble qualities that will allow us to "soar and journey through the expanse of never-ending spiritual worlds." But I recognize that capable is not exactly the same as enable. Can do does not mean did do. For some people learning one virtue could be the work of a lifetime, for others it could mean more than one lifetime. If reincarnation is what someone expects, it might explain why they would seem complacent in the face of death and resist change even when the change would be easy and beneficial. Many people subconsciously think they can put off difficult changes into the next life. Many others consciously come to a point of resistance in their life and give up, literally saying to themselves, "not in this lifetime…"

As there are various religions and numerous belief systems, perhaps what we choose with our gift of free will to hold onto as our core belief is a factor? It seems to me the Bahá'í Faith is a good choice for people who lack the patience to take several lifetimes to accomplish the task of learning the needed lessons from material existence.

Or perhaps it is like what a friend with experience in past life regression once said to me on the subject of reincarnation: "this reality is like a school for souls, if you learned nothing, you have to repeat the grade. If you learned the things you need, you get to the next grade. If you learned everything, you get offered a staff position."

If you believe in materialism, when you die, you expect to become nothing. If you believe in reincarnation, when you die you expect to get another chance, taking with you what you already learned…

If you are a Bahá'í, when you die, you are expected to take the virtues that you have acquired and mature into a spiritual being.

Well, that's another way to think about who wins and who loses in life…

Chapter Two

OUR PLACE IN THE WORLD

When we meet someone for the first time, it usually isn't long before the conversation turns to "what do you do for a living?" This is because people have a deep subconscious need to figure out your social status in the group, and your work is an easy way to pigeonhole you. Social status is defined as the relative respect, competence, and deference accorded to individuals, groups, and organizations in a society. At its core, status is about who is thought to be comparatively "better" – not just economically, but on many more subtle levels too, that together convey the sense that the way of life enjoyed by the high status are to be emulated.

These beliefs about who is "better" or "worse" need to be broadly shared among members of a society if that society is to remain stable. As such, high-status members of the hierarchy, the ones who get to "call the shots," decide who is worthy, and who "deserve" access to valuable resources will go to extreme lengths of deception, coercion, and outright violent persecution to prevent their status in the system from changing. When recalcitrant members of the group agitate for systemic changes, the elites tend to view it as a dangerous revolutionary act. To prevent such situations from arising, elites will use shared cultural beliefs to uphold systems of social stratification by making inequality in society appear natural and fair. Another tactic is to target "outsiders" and shift the blame for inequality to convenient scapegoats.

Status hierarchies appear to be universal across human societies, affording valued benefits such as better health, social approval, resources, influence, and personal freedom to those who occupy the higher rungs while justifying not only the present inequality, but also suppression of any incipient change. Superficially, status hierarchies use the possession of status symbols to reinforce the "ladder for success." These symbols serve as cues people can use to determine how much status a person holds and show how by acquiring these symbols they can move up the status ladder. Such symbols can include possession of not just material objects, but socially valuable attributes, like being conventionally beautiful. This is why plastic surgery for some is seen as an "investment." The same holds true for investing in having a "money-making" degree in a field you don't really care about. In a highly materialistic society, this is what the "rungs" of the ladder of success look like.

In very materialistic social status systems, wealth and the display of it through conspicuous consumption are the most common indicators of status. In extreme subcultures such as criminal organizations or investment banking getting and keeping wealth is the only rule there is (and not getting caught). Status consciousness comprises the psychological world most people live in during their waking hours. How to move up the ladder preoccupies the entire lifetimes of all too many people. Success or failure in this regard rules their emotional world. Ironically, a sudden improvement in social status can lead to a person being unable to handle their new situation. There are too many stories about lottery winners ruining their lives to even outline just a few and do justice to the intricacies of each, so let me just pick one for illustration.

Don McNay is a financial consultant to lottery winners and the author of *Life Lessons from the Lottery*. In an interview for *Time* magazine, McNay says, "It's upheaval that they're not ready for. It's the curse of the lottery because it made their lives worse instead of improving them." In particular, he remembers the story of Jack Whittaker, who said of winning the lottery, "I wish that we had torn the ticket up".

Jack Whittaker was already a millionaire when he won an additional $315 million in a lottery in West Virginia in 2002. The then-55-year-old West Virginia construction company president was declared bankrupt about four years later. The slide began with Whittaker being robbed of $545,000 in cash while sitting in his car outside a strip club just months after winning the lottery. He soon lost a daughter and a granddaughter to drug overdoses, which he blamed on the curse of the Powerball win. "My granddaughter is dead because of the money," he told an ABC news interviewer. "You know, my wife had said she wished that she had torn the ticket up. Well, I wish that we had torn the ticket up, too." Whittaker reflects that, "I just don't like Jack Whittaker. I don't like the hard heart I've got. I don't like what I've become."

"He's the last person I would have prototyped for going completely crazy but he did," McNay told *Time*. "No question it was because he won the lottery." But it could be any sudden increase in status (not just winning the lottery) that knocks someone for a loop and drives them to undertake behavior that make "their lives worse instead of improving them." The underlying reason for this is not just that the person is not "ready" for the suddenness of the change, rather it is that the change forces them to confront the fact that the values of the status system do not conform to their internal reality.

Status systems in general will only allow material measurements of success, the better to control who is esteemed, of course. Internal qualities are a bit hard to quantify, but sometimes status systems can use non-physical qualities to buttress the logic of the hierarchy as it stands. In communist states, they value "purity of thought." In religious states, it's "righteousness," and in capitalist states, it is something called, "entrepreneurship."

When someone is hypnotized by the social status system to blindly seek the next rung on the "success" ladder, it is easier to not look around or feel a need to "smell the flowers." When suddenly you have access to all the "things" that you were told would make you happy and successful, but slowly you realize they didn't, a crisis can occur.

The so-called lottery winners' curse is just a rapid onset version of the mental malady I treated in China. It is not the suddenness of the wealth that is the issue, it is that it didn't fulfill its promise and they don't know what to do next. So, sometimes people do extreme things. I have also seen people who were already happy, who understood the connection between physical, emotional and mental fulfillment and how this relates to their spiritual development, handle sudden financial gains with no problem whatsoever. The difference is resonance.

The happy people were already in resonance with their material, emotional and psychic environment; a sudden increase in any particular area only increased the overall power of their lives. They are loving, unselfish people to start with and could share whatever unexpected fortune came their way. Being "in resonance" with the life energy around them, these people were able to benefit many others around them, and the change had no ill psychological effects on themselves. Their secret was they were willing to SHARE their good fortune.

The unhappy were already not resonating with their life situation, unfulfilled in being themselves, always seeking "success" as something external. A sudden increase in energy in a part of their life only increases the emptiness they feel inside, causing them to make it even more "about them." As this feeling of being unfulfilled is turned up and finds no outlet, it soon becomes unbearable. The answer lies within…

The answer is to fine-tune one's perception to what is true to one's inner experience and not the fabrication of the social status system that you were born into. If you believe your happiness must depend on something happening in the external world, you are a slave to the vagaries of this contingent universe. If the "thing" that you need, doesn't happen, you can't be happy. If it happens, you will be confronted with a version of the "lottery winners' curse." Or you will simply move onto the next "thing" that will make you happy. The metaphysical realization that comes from truly understanding what a human being is will tell you that it is not out in the world that you will find the thing to complete you, rather it is being who you are from the core of your being that brings wholeness to your world. The human being flowers into the spiritual being, but the beauty that grows into view was already in the seed.

The art of bringing bud to flower is an apt metaphor for the process I am describing here. Like the gardener who must provide the proper environment for his plants to bloom, we must also be careful to attune to the needs of our spiritual self. Negative fixations on outside events or internal states of mind should be avoided. If negative people insist on making themselves a part of your life, treat their negativity as fertilizer for your spiritual flowers. Try not to make overly violent stories a part of your entertainment. Repeated exposure to scenes of violence will create a form of desensitization that hardens the spirit. If the spirit is trapped in a shell that is too dense, it will require much more energy to break into flower.

Resonating with the planet

Did you know the planet is constantly resonating? You might recall in September of 2016, seismometers began lighting up around East Asia. From South Korea to Russia to Japan, geophysical instruments recorded squiggles as seismic waves passed through and shook the ground. It looked as if an earthquake with a magnitude of 5.2 had just happened. But the ground shaking had originated at North Korea's nuclear weapons test site. Like a police examiner scrutinizing skid marks to figure out who was at fault in a car crash, researchers analyze seismic waves to determine if they come from a natural earthquake or an artificial explosion, and tease out details such as whether the blast was nuclear and how big it was. Test after test, seismologists are improving their understanding of North Korea's nuclear weapons program.

But this is not the kind of resonance I am talking about. The resonance I am thinking of comes from a power much greater than a nuclear explosion. The combined power of all nuclear blasts since that first one in the New Mexico desert until today all combined together... does not even come close to the energy generated by the planet in the form of lightning strikes in a single day. An average lightning bolt has many times the concentrated power of the bomb dropped on Hiroshima, and about 100 lightning bolts strike the Earth's surface every second. That is approximately eight million per day and three billion each year. Each bolt can contain up to one billion volts of electricity.

In 1952, the German physicist W.O. Schumann hypothesized that there must be measurable electromagnetic waves in the atmosphere that were the global resonances generated and excited by lightning discharges in the cavity between the surface of the earth and the ionosphere.

According to NASA, the ionosphere is an abundant layer of electrons, ionized atoms, and molecules that stretches from approximately 30 miles above the surface of the earth to the edge of space, at about 600 miles. This dynamic region grows and shrinks and divides into sub-regions based on solar conditions and is a critical link in the chain of sun-earth interactions. It is the ionosphere's unique properties that make global telecommunications even possible, as otherwise any signal would simply disperse into space preventing all over the horizon transmissions.

Two years later, in 1954, Schumann and H.L. König confirmed this hypothesis by successfully detecting resonances in the ionosphere at a main frequency of 7.83 Hz. The "Schumann resonance" was officially established and since then many biologists have theorized that due to the proven effect that electromagnetic fields have on the biological circuitry of the mammalian brain, this frequency could have an effect on human consciousness. Furthermore, the pervasive nature of the resonance means it would have functioned as a kind of "tuning fork for life." In other words, the background frequency of the planet has been influencing the evolution of life from its very beginnings.

Recent discoveries that spiders use the Earth's electromagnetic field to fly further prove that the linkage between life and this field is ancient. Spiders have no wings, but they can take to the air nonetheless. Whenever they feel the need, spiders will climb to an exposed point, raise their abdomens to the sky, extrude strands of silk, and float away. This behavior is called ballooning. It might be a way to flee from predators and competitors or it could a chance to land on another patch of ground with abundant resources. Whatever the reason, it's clearly an effective means of travel. Spiders have been found two-and-a-half miles up in the air, and thousands of miles out to sea. It was commonly believed that ballooning works because the silk catches on the wind, dragging the spider with it. But that theory never entirely made sense, especially since spiders have only been found to balloon during light winds. Spiders don't shoot silk from their abdomens, and it is unlikely that gentle breezes would serve to yank the threads out into sails. No one is known to have wind tunnel-tested spiders, but it seems improbable that wind alone would ever be able to carry the larger species aloft, or even to generate the high accelerations for arachnid takeoff. Darwin himself found the rapidity of the spiders' flight to be "quite unaccountable" and its cause to be "inexplicable."

But Erica Morley and Daniel Robert finally found the real explanation. The duo working at the University of Bristol has shown that spiders can sense the Earth's electric field, and use it to launch themselves into the air. The idea of flight by electrostatic repulsion was first proposed in the early 1800s. Peter Gorham, a physicist, resurrected the idea in 2013, and showed that it was mathematically plausible. Now, Morley and Robert have proved that Nature has been using it with spiders for millions of years. First, they showed that spiders can detect electric fields by putting arachnids on vertical strips of cardboard in the center of a plastic box, and then generating an electric field between the floor and ceiling of similar strengths to what the spiders would experience outdoors. These fields ruffle tiny sensory hairs on the spiders' feet, known as trichobothria, via a static electric charge. "It's like when you rub a balloon and hold it up to your hairs," Morley says.

In response, the spiders performed a set of movements called tiptoeing where they stand on the ends of their legs and stick their abdomens in the air. "That behavior is only ever seen before ballooning," Morley explains. Many of the spiders actually managed to take off from the cardboard strip despite being inside a closed box with no airflow within at all. When Morley turned off the electric field inside the boxes, the ballooning spiders dropped back down. The discovery made headlines around the world and managed to break out of the "Science" section due to its connection to something most people are familiar with – the scene of thousands of gossamer strands of spider silk draping across forests and fields.

As far back as is known, the earth's electromagnetic field has been permeating all living things with this natural frequency, a pulsation of 7.83 Hz. Some have called this the earth's heartbeat. The ancient Indian Rishis referred to it this as "OHM," or the incarnation of pure sound. Coincidentally, the frequency of 7.83 Hz happens to be a very powerful frequency used with brain wave entrainment. It is associated with low levels of alpha and the upper range of theta brainwaves. This frequency has also been shown to cause increased HGH (human growth hormone) levels and induce higher cerebral blood flow levels if it is amplified.

However, our level of understanding of the complex interplay between frequency and physical is in its infancy. Even basic theoretical elements such as that lightning causes the Schumann resonance and that it is stable over time have recently been challenged.

On January 31, 2017, for the first time in recorded history, the Schumann resonance was recorded as reaching frequencies of 36+ Hz. It was considered an anomaly when in 2014 this frequency rose from its usual 7.83 Hz to somewhere in the 15-25 Hz levels. The leap from 7.83 Hz to 36+ Hz is rather astounding. That's more than a five-fold increase in resonant frequency levels. What does this mean to us as inhabitants of Mother Earth?

It has long been suspected that the magnetic field of the earth can impact human consciousness and create disturbances in it, but could it be vice versa as well? Particularly during these current times of high anxiety, tension, and passion, could it be that the increase in the resonance is linked to the charged political, social, and economic environments we are creating? Could the drastic rise in frequency have something to do with Donald Trump's election a couple months before it was measured?

Or is it something rather opposite to this supposition? As we know, the higher the frequency, the more highly diversified the information those frequencies carry. Could it be that as the resonance in the electromagnetic field is rising, our brains are being enabled to pick up greater frequencies that are higher than the stressed state of high beta? If so, is there a range of brain frequencies above the scale of high beta that, instead of being associated with being over-aroused and unbalanced, is associated with a brain that is more aware, conscious, and creative?

Perhaps the higher resonance means we are on the verge of a great evolutionary jump. Perhaps the planet is assisting us in lifting the veil, and enabling us see our true nature. Certainly if we collectively take the four steps and one giant leap into a metaphysical perspective, then we can see, remember, and awaken to who we truly are: one life energy in many souls. Then it will be easy, obvious even, for human beings to move from a state of "struggle for survival" to one of "drive to thrive." But first, we have to learn to be less afraid. More willing to share. We need to change the belief that when we die, we DIE. Indeed, we must learn to move beyond belief altogether. In the physical world, let science be the guide. In the emotional world, let the "golden rule" rule. In your intellectual world, find unity in truth through a diversity of views. Then it will be natural and easy to plug your energy into the world energy.

For evidence that strongly suggests human consciousness can have a direct, measurable and tangible impact in changing the world, I refer you to Dr. Kathy J. Forti, a clinical psychologist and author of the book, "Fractals of God." She speculates that an increase in the resonant frequencies of the planet can be likened to a measurement of humanity's collective consciousness level, and it could be pointing directly to an oncoming human evolutionary change. According to Forti, the frequency of 7.83 Hz, the one that as far as anyone knows has been what life has evolved within, is a mixture of the alpha and theta states, a "relaxed, yet dreamy sort of a neutral idling state waiting for something to happen." Moving beyond those states into the theta range bring about faster, more alert beta frequencies. Forti further argues that if we take this rise in frequency to be a sign of a rise in our collective consciousness, then it "correlates with slowly waking up cognitively."

The use of trans-cranial magnetic stimulation (TMS) in medicine shows how much we can be affected by a change in the magnetic fields around us. In TMS, a coil is used to cause electric current to flow in a small region of the brain via electromagnetic induction. During a TMS procedure, a magnetic field generator is placed near the head of the person receiving the treatment. The coil is connected to a pulse generator, called the "stimulator," that delivers a controlled electric current to the coil.

TMS is used diagnostically to measure the connection between the central nervous system and skeletal muscle to evaluate damage in a wide variety of disease states, including those associated with stroke, multiple sclerosis, amyotrophic lateral sclerosis, movement disorders, and motorneuron diseases. It is also used to treat neuropathic pain, for which there are currently no other effective treatments. TMS has been found to be effective for treating depressive disorders. In 2008, the US Food and Drug Administration authorized the use of TMS as an effective treatment for clinical depression, and the Royal Australia and New Zealand College of Psychiatrists endorsed TMS for treatment resistant depression in 2013.

However, using the logic of Occam's razor, the problem-solving principle that, when presented with competing hypothetical answers to a problem, one should select the one that makes the fewest assumptions, we might first consider a physical cause to the rise in planetary resonance. Is it possible that the change is caused by human activity on the material plane and is not related to any influence our collective consciousness might be exerting? Patrick Roddie and Peter A. Kirby, both geoengineering researchers, have written about their knowledge of technology that has the power to change weather systems through sending massive charges of electromagnetic energy into the ionosphere. Could this technology be doing something to the Schumann resonance?

This technology comes in two parts. First, the sky has to be filled with micro-particulates of barium, aluminum, strontium and other materials of a similar nature. Then when sufficient electromagnetic energy is applied to the particles floating in the atmosphere and the masses of air associated to said particles are moved around, whole weather systems can theoretically be manipulated.

There is a patent for what Roddie and Kirby called a "System for Changing the Weather." Alphabet, the parent company of Google (and many other lesser known ventures) filed US patent #4,686,605 with the much longer and less revealing title of "Method and Apparatus for Altering a Region in the Earth's Atmosphere Ionosphere and/or Magnetosphere." The patent has been a point of reference for those who argue that the sky above us has already been regularly sprayed with micro-particulates for some time. In the patent, technical aspects of how electromagnetic energy can be beamed into the atmosphere and how this can be directed to affect stratospheric level metallic aerosols to change the weather is presented in clear scientific language that hides any negative effects and only stress "positive" effects.

From the patent:

"Weather modification is possible by, for example, altering upper atmosphere wind patterns or altering solar absorption patterns by constructing one or more plumes of atmospheric particles which will act as a lens or focusing device. Also as alluded to earlier, molecular modifications of the atmosphere can take place so that positive environmental effects can be achieved...

It has also been proposed to release large clouds of barium in the magnetosphere so that photoionization will increase the cold plasma density, thereby producing electron precipitation through enhanced whistler-mode interactions."

So, the idea is that from a very high altitude a plane large enough to carry out long-term spraying of "large clouds of barium" (and some proprietary blend of "chemicals"), like a large jetliner, would fly over large areas of the sky and spray out metallic particles that would act like volcanic ash. These long thick trails would slowly spread from the spray planes and mix into the air leaving a faint haze that never fully dissipates....

Yeah, we have all seen something like that... Some "conspiracy theorists" call them chemtrails.

Once the skies become sufficiently electromagnetically active, entire weather systems can be guided by "HAARP"-type facilities that are on the ground.

The "High Frequency Active Auroral Research Program (HAARP)" is a US high-powered, high-frequency transmitter based in Alaska used to "study" the ionosphere. The most prominent instrument at HAARP is the Ionospheric Research Instrument (IRI), a high-powered radio frequency transmitter facility operating in the high frequency (HF) band. The IRI is used to temporarily excite a limited area of the ionosphere. Other instruments, such as a VHF and a UHF radar, a fluxgate magnetometer, a digisonde (an ionospheric sounding device), and an induction magnetometer, are used to study the physical processes that occur in the excited region.

Work on the HAARP facility began in 1993. The current working IRI was completed in 2007; its prime contractor was BAE Systems Advanced Technologies. In 2008, public inquiries revealed the cost of HAARP was over $250 million in tax-funded construction and operating costs. HAARP became a target of "conspiracy theorists," who claim that it is used to "weaponize" weather. Mainstream scientists emerged to say that advocates of this theory are uninformed, and that their claims fall well outside the abilities of the facility, if not "beyond the scope of natural science." However, more people became aware of HAARP as a result.

In May 2014, it was announced that the HAARP program would be permanently shut down later in the year. After discussions between the parties, ownership of the facility and its equipment was transferred to the University of Alaska Fairbanks in August 2015.

Because chemtrails and HAARP are two sides of one coin, "conspiracy theorist" was also applied to people who expressed concern over the various effects from "molecular modifications of the atmosphere" via spraying of chemtrails. These claimed effects range from strange patterns of tree deaths to Morgellons disease, a poorly understood condition characterized by small fibers or other particles emerging from skin sores. People with this condition often report feeling as if something were crawling on or stinging their skin. Many mainstream doctors see Morgellons as a mental delusion and if the patient links it with chemtrail poisoning they will treat it with antidepressants or even anti-psychotic drugs. Others think the symptoms are related to an infectious or allergic process in skin cells.

Meanwhile most mainstream scientists simply refused to acknowledge chemtrails exists. Despite obvious visual difference, they continue to claim what is being observed are just a kind of very persistent water vapor condensation trail...

However, one brave scientist has spoken out.

Marvin Herndon, an American interdisciplinary scientist who earned his BA in physics in 1970 from the University of California at San Diego and his PhD in nuclear chemistry in 1974 from Texas A&M University, supports the argument that chemtrails are real. Herndon is highly esteemed in his profession, and has worked extensively with famous scientists such as geochemist Hans Suess and Manhattan Project physical chemist Harold Urey. In private life, he is known and respected for being a politically active citizen.

Herndon asserts that the "chemtrails" so often seen polluting our skies and fouling our biosphere is the first part of a hidden in plain sight weather manipulation system, with HAARP being the second operational part. He has found strong physical evidence that chemtrails consist of coal fly ash. Since June of 2015 Dr. Herndon has published eight scientific journal articles exposing the currently ongoing, uncontrolled geoengineering experiments taking place daily above our heads. In the course of his investigations, he has found that the chemical signatures of chemtrail spray and coal fly ash are indistinguishable.

For thousands of years, coal fly ash has been used in cements. Today coal fly ash is mostly used in construction materials such as roadbeds and high-quality cements. Coal fly ash enables cementitious building materials to dry faster and set stronger. But only about 45% of the national coal fly ash production is used up in these purposes. In the past, most of it was buried as a toxic waste, to the great expense of the power industry.

In attempts to turn their lemons into lemonade, since 1967 international fly ash utilization symposia have been held. Powerful organizations such as: the Calgary Fly Ash Research Group, the Western Fly Ash Research Development and Data Center, the Edison Electric Institute, the Electric Power Research Institute, the American Public Power Association, the Department of the Interior, and the Department of Energy have historically been very serious about utilizing coal fly ash. Today the biggest dog in the space appears to be an industry group called The American Coal Ash Association.

There is quite a historical precedent for the use of coal fly ash in weather modification and the atmospheric sciences. Many military men have claimed that the smoke from exploded bombs causes precipitation. The early American meteorologist James Pollard Espy (AKA 'The Storm King') claimed that forest fires caused rain to fall. The Nobel Prize-winning weather modifier Irving Langmuir worked with fine particle oil smokes during WWII. There are some geoengineers now arguing that since stratospheric masses of volcanic ash spewing from a fiery volcano can reflect sunlight back into space and therefore cool the planet, we could spray a lot more of a similar substance in the sky, and that might save us from the dread of global warming. Many, if not all of the things geoengineers say they want to spray is exactly what is in coal fly ash – silica, sulphates, salts, and aluminum.

If coal fly ash is being used to spray over-populated areas as chemtrails, the practice would have a precedent in water fluoridation programs that are common worldwide. When our local water district adds fluoride to the pipes, it is not the natural chalky mineral fluoride most people think it is. What is put in the water is an industrial waste product called hydrofluosilicic acid which, if the population was not forced to ingest in what we are told are "safe diluted amounts," would be classified as a toxic waste in its normal form and be very expensive to get rid of. Instead, in the name of "dental hygiene," governments use your tax money to dispose of industrial hydrofluosilicic acid by adding it to the drinking water supply.

Most people never wonder why we need to add fluoride to the drinking water when it is already in most over-the-counter toothpaste which would have a much more direct benefit to dental health. While there is no warning label for what is added to the water, there is one for what is added to the toothpaste. If you look carefully, most packages have a small print warning that reads along the lines of, "If you accidentally swallow more than used for brushing, seek professional help or contact a poison control center immediately." None of the caveats that began appearing on toothpaste tubes in 1991 so candidly broached the risks of ingesting too much fluoride as the current one that advises seeking out poison control. General warnings on toothpaste products that display the American Dental Association seal of approval used to only caution, "Don't Swallow — Use only a pea-sized amount for children under six," and "Children under 6 should be supervised while brushing with any toothpaste to prevent swallowing." The word "poison" wasn't used, but more research on the toxic nature of fluoride led to the current warning.

"When I receive the fluoride here, it has a skull-and-bones on it," Regina Miskewitz says of the containers of the chemical she works with at the Princeton, N.J., laboratory of Arm & Hammer products, where she is director of research and development for oral and personal care. "If a child ingested a whole tube of toothpaste, he should be taken right to the emergency room and he would either get his stomach pumped or get some kind of antidote." I suspect under the Trump administration, the warning will soon be deleted.

Though HAARP has been officially transferred to civilian control, it is suspected there are now more such facilities in the US whose locations are considered classified. What is known is that such sites have been seen on Google Earth in Russia, China and Australia. Peter Kirby said that if two HAARP-type facilities are injecting electromagnetic energy into the atmosphere at once, it can create a distinct wave interference pattern in the sprayed aerosols. The result would be a fight between the different beams to see which could exert more power on the charged particles in the clouds.

However, after carefully considering the possible effect of all suspected HAARP-type activity and their estimated collective power levels, I find it highly unlikely they can be the cause of altering something once thought as unchangeable as the planet's background resonance. However, since very little is understood about how interference patterns from different HAARP-type beams might affect the ionosphere, the use of multiple, possibly conflicting systems, might be an unforeseen factor. Recall how in the movie, "The Ghostbusters," the team was told to "never cross the beams" of their electromagnetic guns. And when they did, all hell breaks loose...

The application of "conspiracy theorists" label to people who argue that chemtrails and HAARP represent the twin components of a weather weapon is itself a social-political weapon. There is little question in my mind that there is a direct link between why published coal fly ash storage costs from the major steelmakers began to disappear from their account books, and the start of what some have called "the new Manhattan Project." The still-unanswered question is whether the change in the planet's resonance is natural or man-made or something in between.

Having considered the possibility that the increase in the planetary resonance is the result of human tampering with the ionosphere, we might consider the effect of a less physically intrusive technological advancement that has nonetheless had a profound effect on human consciousness – the Internet. Like geoengineering, the Internet grew out of military roots. The origins of the Internet date back to research commissioned by the Advanced Research Projects Administration (ARPANET) for an early packet-switching network and the first network to implement the protocol suite TCP/IP. Both technologies became the technical foundation of the Internet. The ARPANET was initially funded by the Advanced Research Projects Agency (ARPA) of the United States

Department of Defense. The military need in the 1960s was to build a robust, fault-tolerant communications system with distributed computer networks that would increase the chance of the system's survival in a nuclear attack.

The precursor network, ARPANET, initially served as a backbone for interconnection of regional academic and military networks in the 1980s. With additional funding from the National Science Foundation, the ARPANET was allowed to take on an additional role as a new public "inter-networks" backbone for academic and commercial networks to link to. Soon private funding for commercial extensions saw a massive proliferation of online businesses, culminating in the "Dot.com" boom and subsequent collapse in 2000.

The emergence of the internet as we know it came after years of worldwide participation in the development of new networking technologies, and the merger of many networks. The linking of commercial networks and enterprises across national borders by the early 1990s marks the beginning of the transition to the modern Internet, and generated a sustained exponential growth in many related industries such as search engines and mobile networks. As generations of institutional, personal, and mobile computers were connected to the network, it created new industries such as social media, crypto currencies, and online payments. Although the Internet was widely used by academia since the 1980s, commercialization and wide acceptance by the public has led to its incorporation into virtually every aspect of modern life.

This deep and profound penetration of the Internet has led some observers to call the world-wide web a kind of primitive global neural net. More cynical critics of technology see a NSA tool to get people to spy on themselves. Security expert, Steve Rambam who specializes in Internet privacy cases, believe the Internet has created a social reality where privacy no longer exists. Rambam is fond of saying, "Privacy is dead – get over it." In fact, it has been proven that social media companies use the appeal of using their online services to harvest personal information for resale purposes.

On the other hand, in his essay "The Value of Privacy", security expert Bruce Schneier says, "Privacy protects us from abuses by those in power, even if we're doing nothing wrong at the time of surveillance." It is general knowledge in the post-Edward Snowden era that the National Security Agency (NSA) spies on everyone in America, and has plenty of bandwidth for the rest of the world too. The Utah Data Center, also known as the Comprehensive National Cybersecurity Initiative Data Center (CNCI Center) is a data storage facility for the United States intelligence community that is designed to store data estimated to be on the order of eight exabytes or larger. Allegedly, all words ever spoken by human beings could be stored in approximately five exabytes of data.

The stated purpose of creating this massive storage facility is to support the Comprehensive National Cybersecurity Initiative, although the precise mission of the CNCI is classified. What is known is that the NSA leads operations at the facility as the executive agent for the Director of National Intelligence. The center is located at Camp Williams near Bluffdale, Utah, between Utah Lake and Great Salt Lake, and was completed in May 2014 at a cost of $1.5 billion.

The Internet fulfills the prophecy of the "global village" that Marshall McLuhan popularized in his book *Understanding Media* (1964). McLuhan described how the globe has been contracted into a village by electronic communications and the instantaneous movement of information from every quarter to every point at the same time. The full technology fulfillment was decades away when he wrote his prediction, but we can justly say in many ways, the "village" has arrived. Even as social media has eroded the traditional broadcast media's ability to offer controlled narratives, they themselves are being challenged by "independent media" producers who are using new distributed technologies to directly reach their audience.

Even as technology has brought us unprecedented ways of destroying one another, and given government ever greater means to intrude on and monitor the public, it has also given people new ways to connect and organize. Another sign of technology's doubled-edged nature is the rise of cryptocurrencies. Born from encryption technology invented during wartime and nurtured by methodologies that border on spycraft, cryptos promise to be a game changer in the balance of power between centralized banking cabals run by the elites and average people. This is because "distributed ledger" technology, on which cryptocurrency is based, creates crypt-currency collectively, at a rate which is defined when the system is created and which is publicly known. In centralized banking and economic systems such as the Federal Reserve System, corporate boards or governments control the supply of currency by printing units of fiat money or demanding additions to digital banking ledgers. "Fiat" is Latin for "I say so." Put simply, this is why Ford said people would take to the streets if they really understood the banking system. The money that people work so hard to earn is simply created out of thin air by bankers when they lend it out. Let me repeat that: They lend you money that you create by borrowing it.

The underlying technical system for the "first blockchain" upon which the decentralized crypt-currency known as Bitcoin is run was created by the group or individual known as Satoshi Nakamoto. The Bitcoin blockchain released in 2009 was the first public decentralized crypt-currency. The code served as a model for other developers and since then numerous other cryptocurrencies have been created. These are frequently called alternative coins – "altcoins."

Despite the Internet being used by governments and corporations to track individuals, the rise of sophisticated encryption technology for personal use, proliferation of reputation networks, monetization of blockchain network data in the form of cryptocurrencies, and the reality of a mini super-computer in your hand, has seen the average individual "villager" become much more empowered. As McLuhan predicted when distance becomes meaningless and information flows more easily, what was once possible to keep secret and controlled will quickly become known by many. It is getting harder and harder for the "facilitator" class to work their media magic programming and get the "resource" class to respond in the desired direction. Witness the current controversy over media favoritism in the last presidential election and both sides charging the other of using "fake news." It is part of the historical record that many members of the mass media supported Hillary Clinton, and tried to present an "inevitable" quality to her campaign. The shock and apparent disgust they presented as it became clear Trump would win is there for everyone to see.

However, despite claiming the populist mantle in his fight with the corporate media, Trump is not what he so loudly proclaims himself to be, a fighter for the "working (white) man." Rather like how we see competing HAARP type systems in the sky jostling to control events best left to their own natural process, what we are witnessing in US politics nowadays is competing factions within the social-status system exerting their influence on the electorate. Both parties are run by the "facilitator" class on behalf of the "owners" of the country, and all you have to look at is who Trump's appointments are to know that there is very little difference. You see a bunch of Wall Street types, mostly from one company. This is how he is going to "Make America Great Again" for the "owners" of which he is a proud and life-long member.

I do not despair at the rise of Donald Trump to the American presidency only because in my view, his policies are going to quickly prove unworkable and will result in an electoral repudiation of epic proportions. At present, his administration is already stimulating progressive forces as never before. But my intuition tells me that the rise in the planet's resonance is not only indicating a potential quickening in human consciousness, but also a dire warning from the non-human living energies that surrounds us. Perhaps the Natural World is providing a warning sign that humanity and the other creatures it shares the planet with are one, intimately connected and reciprocal, and both are in crisis.

For an example of a growing ecological crisis, we can look at the Pacific Ocean. The Great Pacific garbage patch is reaching frightening proportions. Also described as the Pacific trash vortex, it is a gyre of marine debris particles in the central North Pacific Ocean discovered around 1986. Located roughly between 135°W to 155°W and 35°N to 42°N, the patch extends over an indeterminate area of widely varying range depending on the degree of plastic concentration used to define the affected area. The patch is made up of high concentrations of plastic fragments, chemical sludge, and other debris that have been trapped by the currents of the North Pacific Gyre. This swirling pile of trash in the Pacific Ocean is growing faster than expected and was recently measured at three times the size of France.

According to a three-year study published in Scientific Reports, the mass of garbage is about 1.6 million square kilometers in size – up to 16 times bigger than previous estimates. Ghost nets, or discarded fishing nets, make up almost half the 80,000 metric tons of garbage floating at sea, and researchers believe that around 20% of the total volume of trash is debris from the 2011 Japanese tsunami.

Plastics, made from the byproducts of oil production that were once treated as industrial waste, began its rise to the billion dollars industry we see today in the 1950s. Plastic pollution is the accumulation of plastic products in the environment that adversely affects wildlife, wildlife habitat, or humans. Plastic pollutants are categorized into micro, meso, or macro debris, based on size. Being inexpensive and durable, plastic is in high demand. However, the chemical structure of most plastics renders them resistant to many natural processes of degradation and as a result they are slow to degrade. Together, these two factors have led to a high prominence of plastic pollution in the environment.

Plastic pollution can afflict land, waterways and oceans. Living organisms, particularly marine animals, can be harmed either by mechanical effects, such as entanglement in plastic objects or ingestion of plastic waste, or exposure to the chemicals within plastics that interfere with their physiology.

This recent news item highlights the urgency of the problem:

"A young male sperm whale washed up dead on the southeastern coast of Spain in February, and now scientists know what killed the animal. During a recent necropsy, investigators discovered nearly 65 lbs. (29 kilograms) of plastic trash crammed into the dead whale's stomach and intestines. A Twitter photo shared by a regional nature conservation agency shows the whale's stomach contents in grim detail... dozens of plastic bags, chunks of mangled rope, glass, a large water container and several sacks of packing materials."

Humans are also affected by plastic pollution, such as through disruption of various hormonal mechanisms. The full impact of plastic infiltration into the biosphere is still unclear...

The deterioration of the natural environment prompted the rise of the modern environmental movement. In 1962, *Silent Spring* by

American biologist Rachel Carson was published. The book cataloged the environmental impacts of the indiscriminate spraying of DDT in the US and questioned the logic of releasing large amounts of chemicals into the environment without fully understanding their effects on human health and ecology. The book suggested that DDT and other pesticides may cause cancer and that their agricultural use was a threat to wildlife, particularly birds.

The resulting public concern led to the creation of the United States Environmental Protection Agency in 1970 which subsequently banned the agricultural use of DDT in the US in 1972. The limited use of DDT in disease vector control continues to this day in certain parts of the world and remains controversial. The book's lasting legacy was to produce a far greater awareness of environmental issues and interest into how people affect the environment.

Along with the new interest in the environment came interest in tackling specific problems such as air pollution, endangered species, and petroleum spills. National pressure groups formed, notably Greenpeace and Friends of the Earth, as well as notable local organizations. However, under heavy propaganda from business groups and right-wing think tanks, polling indicates a precipitous decline in the US public's interest in 19 different areas of environmental concern.

Americans are less likely now to be actively participating in an environmental movement or organization, and more likely to self-identify as "unsympathetic" to environmental issues, than they were in 2000. This is likely a lingering factor of the Great Recession in 2008, but since 2005, the percentage of Americans agreeing that the environment should be given priority over economic growth has dropped 10 points, in contrast, those feeling that growth should be given priority "even if the environment suffers to some extent" has risen 12 percent.

These numbers point to the growing complexity of environmentalism and its relationship to economics, and increasing financial insecurity on the part of the American public. They also point to a decrease in environmental consciousness in general. If fewer people are able to recognize the gravity of the harm being done to the environment than in

2000, we can be sure, the business elites will take this as a sign they can push for more reduction in environmental regulations.

If people awake to our connection to nature, the direct effect will be seen in stronger support for environmental legislation. If people do not awaken, the effect on the biosphere will quickly become clear as we are simply using up what would be "renewable" natural resources, if we used them responsibly, at an alarming rate. A forced awakening in the form of ecological collapse will be brutal if we insist on continuing to sleep. Even now nature is crying for help in the form of mass animal deaths. In recent years, millions of birds, fish, crabs and other small marine life have been turning up dead in massive numbers from the United States, through Europe and down to South America. Scientists and environmental officials have attributed some of the deaths to severe weather, dramatic drops in temperature – even fireworks. However, many reported deaths remain "mysterious."

The rise in the Schumann resonance could be our alarm clock going off, "time to wake up." Or it could be the smoke alarm going off, "the house is on fire!" When human consciousness awakens to its oneness with nature, and our capacity to love each other is more fully realized, human beings will be able to not only heal ourselves but the natural world around us.

Before I move on, let me take a minute to address any Trump supporter who might be reading this book and how what Trump's environmental policies are. Let us quickly review them.

The Trump administration has sought to increase fossil fuel use and scrap environmental regulations which he has often referred to as an impediment to business. Neither Trump nor his former Environmental Protection Agency (EPA) Administrator Scott Pruitt believe carbon dioxide is a primary contributor to global warming. While campaigning Trump had proposed the elimination of the EPA and following his election he proposed a 31% cut to the 2018 EPA budget.

Trump has pulled the United States out of the Paris climate agreement, making it currently the only country on the planet not a signatory. Immediately upon his inauguration, the White House released an "America First Energy Plan," which focused on increasing combustion of fossil fuels without mentioning renewable energy. The plan would limit the EPA's mission of protecting air and water quality.

Within days of taking office he signed executive orders to approve two controversial oil pipelines (one of which has already had a major spill) and to require federal review of the Clean Water Rule and the Clean Power Plan. Trump is calling for more drilling in national parks and has announced plans to open up more federal land and offshore sites for energy development. Trump's plans to allow drilling, in nearly all US waters, is the largest expansion of offshore oil and gas leasing ever proposed.

The administration is re-writing EPA pollution-control policies of chemicals that are known to be serious health risks to make them "more friendly" to the chemical industry. Trump's appointments to key agencies dealing in energy and environmental policy reflected his commitment to deregulation, particularly of the fossil fuel industry. He invited American manufacturers to suggest which regulations should be eliminated, and of the suggestions from industry leaders, nearly half targeted EPA rules.

Often citing questionable or non-existence scientific "facts" to defend his environmental policy, Trump seems to have no understanding of what scientific thinking is. I will close this section with an extended quote that explains it ably.

"Science is more than a body of knowledge; it is a way of thinking. I have a foreboding of an America in my children's or grandchildren's time – when the United States is a service and information economy; when nearly all the key manufacturing industries have slipped away to other countries; when awesome technological powers are in the hands of a very few, and no one representing the public interest can even grasp the issues; when the people have lost the ability to set their own agendas or knowledgeably question those in authority; when, clutching our crystals and nervously consulting our horoscopes, our critical faculties in decline, unable to distinguish between what feels good and what's true, we slide, almost without noticing, back into superstition and darkness. Science is more than a body of knowledge. It's a way of thinking... a way of skeptically interrogating the universe with a fine understanding of human fallibility.

If we are not able to ask skeptical questions, to interrogate those who tell us something is true, to be skeptical of those in authority, then we're up for grabs for the next charlatan, political or religious, who comes ambling along."

Carl Sagan (1934-1996)

Resonating with the universe

Ever notice that when a long-held idea or antiquated system reaches the end of usefulness, and something is desperately needed to replace it, the socio-cultural matrix conjures up what is needed, and what is needed seems to just show up? When the world needed a way to transition out of the current debt-based financial system in the aftermath of the still unwinding 2008 "Great Recession," new cryptocurrencies arrived. When Western natural philosophy was undergoing a much-needed sea change forced upon it by the experimental findings of quantum theory, and simultaneously, facing doubt and uncertainty in the physical explanations of the universe's genesis and structure, Biocentrism, a revolutionary view of the universe, was proposed.

Every now and then a simple yet radical idea shakes the very foundations of knowledge. The startling discovery that the world was not flat challenged and ultimately changed the way people perceived themselves and their relationship with the world. For most humans of the 15th century, the Earth was the center of creation. The sun and moon revolved around us. The Roman Catholic Church condemned Galileo for proposing that the Earth revolved around the sun, and it took Pope John Paul II 350 years to rectify one of the Church's most infamous wrongs in 1992.

With a formal statement at the Pontifical Academy of Sciences, Vatican officials announced the close to a 13-year investigation into the Church's condemnation of Galileo in 1633. The condemnation, which forced the astronomer and physicist to recant his discoveries, also led to Galileo's house arrest for eight years before his death in 1642 at the age of 77.

The psychic blow to our self-importance from losing our perceived place at the "center of creation" was too much for the Catholic Church until... 1992. And even today there is a widespread (and a little thin) belief that the Earth is in reality flat, and there is a global covering up of this fact. Believers of the flat Earth theory think the "ball of rock theory" is nonsense.

While the literal belief in a flat Earth can easily be proven false, the intuitive feeling that "we" should be at the center of things that underlies the desire for such a condition might be truer than "Flat Earthers" ever imagined.

Enter Biocentrism, also referred to as the "Biocentric Universe Theory." Biocentrism was proposed by the renowned scientist Robert Lanza. This theory posits that life and biology are the central pieces to being, reality and the cosmos. In Biocentrism, it is the perceptions by living things that explain how the universe is created and maintained, rather than life coming into being long after the universe is created. Biocentrism builds upon the ideas of quantum physics. While physics is considered essential to the study of the universe and chemistry essential to the study of life, biocentrism puts biology before all other sciences in developing a theory of everything – a theory that scientifically introduces the concept of the living universe.

When describing this theory, Robert Lanza explains that what we call space and time are forms of animal sense perception rather than external physical objects. Understanding this simple yet revolutionary idea provides us with new ways to answer some of the major puzzles of mainstream science. In 2010, Lanza and astronomer Bob Berman published their first book on biocentrism, *Biocentrism: How Life and Consciousness are the Keys to Understanding the True Nature of the Universe*.

The book opened the eyes of readers from all across the globe, providing a new perspective on how the universe came to be. In the past, physics has dominated the topic of the universe in Western science. With biocentrism, Lanza uses biology and astronomy to explain that life is not just an accidental byproduct of the laws of physics. Instead, it suggests the invigorating possibility that consciousness is fundamentally immortal at a higher level of reality and created the universe through fine-tuning the "laws of physics" in order to manifest and evolve physical life in the universe.

In my view, these breakthrough scientific findings are in perfect accordance with the Bahá'í teachings that the cause and reason for material creation is God's plan that mankind should come into existence. The human spirit is therefore more fundamental than material reality and can attain higher levels of reality.

According to biocentrism's view of creation, it is life that creates the universe instead of the other way around. In this paradigm, not only is life not an accidental byproduct of the laws of physics, in biocentrism, the very definition of what is alive is reinterpreted. This mind-bending book takes the reader on a seemingly improbable but ultimately convincing journey through our universe with new insight gained from the viewpoints of an acclaimed biologist and a leading astronomer.

Switching perspective from physics to biology unlocks the cages in which Western science had unwittingly managed to confine itself. The ideas presented in biocentrism challenge convention visions of life, time and space, and even death. At the same time the book argues with vigor against the materialistic worldview that life is merely the activity of an admixture of carbon and a few other elements. The book's summary of the latest breakthroughs in scientific theory that combined form the basis of biocentrism is beginning to emerge as the strong evidence-based argument that religion has previously lacked for its teaching that human life is fundamentally immortal.

This development was anticipated by one of the founding principles of the Bahá'í Faith – the harmony of science and religion. Bahá'ís reject the notion that there is an inherent conflict between science and religion, a notion that became prevalent in intellectual discourse at a time when the very conception of each system of knowledge was far from adequate. This foundational teaching tells us that religion, without science, soon degenerates into superstition and fanaticism, while science without religion becomes merely the instrument of crude materialism.

"Religion," according to the Bahá'í writings, "is the outer expression of the divine reality. Therefore, it must be living, vitalized, moving and progressive. Science is the first emanation from God toward man. All created things embody the potentiality of material perfection, but the power of intellectual investigation and scientific acquisition is a higher virtue specialized to man alone. Other beings and organisms are deprived of this potentiality and attainment."

'Abdu'l-Bahá has described science as the "most noble" of all human virtues and "the discoverer of all things." Science has enabled society to separate fact from conjecture. Further, scientific capabilities – of observing, of measuring, of rigorously testing ideas – have allowed humanity to construct a coherent understanding of the laws and processes governing physical reality, as well as to gain insights into human conduct and the life of society.

This ability to use scientific inquiry to gain insights beyond "science" is exemplified by Lanza and Berman in their followup book, *Beyond Biocentrism, Rethinking Time, Space, Consciousness, and the Illusion of Death*. In it, Lanza and Berman reexamine everything material science thought it knew about life, death, the universe, and the nature of reality itself. The book starts with acknowledging that our existing model of reality is looking increasingly creaky in the face of recent scientific discoveries. Material science tells us with some precision that the universe is 26.8 percent dark matter, 68.3 percent dark energy, and only 4.9 percent ordinary matter, but it must confess that it doesn't really know what dark matter is and knows even less about dark energy. Science is increasingly pointing toward an infinite universe but has no ability to explain what that really means. Concepts such as time, space, and even causality as currently understood are increasingly being demonstrated as meaningless.

Lanza and Berman show that all of material science is based on information passing through our consciousness but material science hasn't the foggiest idea what consciousness is, and it can't explain the linkage between subatomic states and observation by conscious observers. Science as it is now generally understood describes life as a random occurrence in a dead universe but has no real understanding of how life began or why the universe appears to be exquisitely designed for the emergence of life.

Biocentrism theory demands and challenges scientists to fully accept the implications of the latest scientific findings in fields ranging from plant biology and cosmology to quantum entanglement and consciousness. By listening to what the actual science is telling us, it becomes increasingly clear that life and consciousness are fundamental to any true understanding of the universe. This forces a fundamental rethinking of everything we thought we knew about life, death, and our place in the universe.

Of course, someone who has read Tom Campbell's *My Big T.O.E. (Theory of Everything)* and is able to adequately understand the concept of consciousness continuously projecting and receiving a data stream which makes up our consensus reality will recognize the questions raised in biocentrism for what they are – sign posts for what lays ahead. The holy grail of science – generally accepted (by scientists at first, but eventually even schoolchildren) Theory of Everything that will unify general relativity, quantum mechanics, and metaphysics along with the origins of consciousness.

Some critics have labeled biocentrism as a rehashing of "Vitalism," a 19th century belief that living organisms are fundamentally different from non-living entities due to some vital principle, referred to as the "vital spark" which some equate with the soul. In the 18th and 19th century vitalism was debated among biologists who felt that the known mechanics of physics would eventually explain the difference between life and non-life (mechanistic universe) and vitalists who argued that the processes of life could not be reduced to a mechanistic process. Some vitalists proposed testable hypotheses meant to show inadequacies with mechanistic explanations, but these experiments failed to provide support for vitalism, and most biologists of the time considered vitalism refuted by empirical evidence, so it was mostly disregarded as a viable scientific theory. However, if the criteria had been to produce something living from non-living substances instead of something organic from non-organic compounds, the vitalists would have prevailed.

The legacy of this "victory" for the mechanistic universe argument made biology a poor cousin to physics, and took the spiritual and energetic aspects of healing out of mainstream science. Vitalism lives on in many traditional healing practices that posit disease results from some imbalance in vital forces and manipulation of that energy can bring healing. Having experienced qi healing and cultivated qigong myself for many years, and having witnessed various paranormal phenomena, I think perhaps vitalism was rejected prematurely and that many of its ideas can be redeemed in biocentrism.

If the universe is geared to the emergence of life and its evolution, what about intelligent life beyond the Earth? Are human beings alone in the universe? Given the vast amount of time that has passed since the formation of the Milky Way galaxy and the emergence of Homo sapiens is it not logical to assume other intelligent life forms have come before us?

Resonating with the aliens

"Ancient astronauts" or "ancient aliens" theory refers to the idea that intelligent extraterrestrial beings visited Earth and made contact with humans in antiquity and even during prehistoric times. Proponents suggest that this contact influenced the development of modern cultures, technologies, and religions. A common position they argue is that deities from most, if not all, religions are actually extraterrestrial entities perceived by primitive humans as gods, and that advanced technologies were interpreted and recorded in religious texts as evidence of divine power by these early human observers.

The idea that ancient astronauts existed is not taken seriously by most academics, and has received no credible attention in mainstream peer-reviewed studies. Proponents argue that the vested interest of conventional academics and the internal rules of their social status system have created a well-known code of self-censorship among scientific circles regarding any evidence for ancient astronauts or advanced ancient technologies.

Citing circumstantial evidence from documentary gaps in historical and archaeological records, "ancient alien theorists," a popular segment of the "conspiracy theorist" market, have sold a lot of books and continue to generate interest in the form of TV shows and documentaries. Besides citing (saying?) that absent or incomplete explanations of historical or archaeological data point to the existence of ancient "contact," evidence in the form of archaeological artifacts that they deem anachronistic, or beyond the accepted technical capabilities of the historical cultures with which they are associated, is a popular device used by believers of the theory. These are sometimes referred to as "out-of-place artifacts" (OOPART); and include artwork and legends which are interpreted in a modern sense as depicting extraterrestrial contact or technologies.

Conventional scholars have responded that gaps in contemporary knowledge are not evidence of the existence of ancient astronauts, and that advocates have not provided any convincing anecdotal or physical evidence of an artifact that might conceivably be the product of alien contact. According to astrophysicist Carl Sagan, "In the long litany of 'ancient astronaut' pop archaeology, the cases of apparent interest have perfectly reasonable alternative explanations, or have been misreported, or are simple prevarications, hoaxes and distortions".

However, in their 1966 book *Intelligent Life in the Universe*, Sagan, in collaboration with astrophysicist I. S. Shklovsk, devoted a chapter to arguments that scientists and historians should seriously consider the possibility that extraterrestrial contact might in fact have occurred during recorded history (while first noting these ideas were speculative and unproven).

Shklovski and Sagan argued that sub-light speed interstellar travel by extraterrestrial life was a high likelihood when considering technologies that were established or feasible by humans in the late 1960s, when they, writing their book, were already spawning theoretical technologies like those in the "Star Trek" TV series. Given the estimated age of the universe, the theoretically arrived-at number of technologically advanced civilizations that might have come before the birth of our solar system is rather large. So why have we still not detected any sign of such alien intelligence?

The idea of searching for extraterrestrial intelligence (SETI) within the solar system was first proposed in 1896, when Nikola Tesla suggested that an extreme version of his wireless electrical transmission system could be used to contact beings on Mars. In 1899, while conducting experiments at his Colorado Springs experimental station, he thought he had detected a signal from that planet since an odd repetitive static signal seemed to cut off when Mars set in the night sky. Analysis of Tesla's research has ranged from suggestions that Tesla detected something local, he misunderstood the new technology he was working with, to claims that Tesla may have been observing signals from Marconi's European radio experiments and even that he picked up naturally occurring Jovian plasma torus signals.

In the early 1900s, Guglielmo Marconi, Lord Kelvin and David Peck Todd, also stated their belief that radio could be used to contact Martians, with Marconi stating that his stations had also picked up potential Martian signals. The public interest was aroused to such a degree that when on August 21–23, 1924, Mars entered an opposition closer to Earth than at any time in the century before or the next 80 years, there was a call in United States to widely promote a "National Radio Silence Day" during the 36-hour period, calling for all radios to quiet for five minutes on the hour, every hour. At the United States Naval Observatory, a radio receiver was lifted 3 kilometers (1.9 miles) above the ground in a dirigible tuned to a wavelength between 8 and 9 km, using a "radio-camera" developed at Amherst College by Charles Francis Jenkins.

The seriousness with which the government considered the program can be seen by their choice of top scientist David Peck Todd to lead it with the assistance of top military personnel. His military assistant on the task was Admiral Edward W. Eberle (Chief of Naval Operations), and he was assigned William F. Friedman (chief cryptographer of the United States Army) to translate any potential Martian messages. It was reported to the public that nothing was heard, and the hype was quickly forgotten... until Sunday, October 30, 1938.

That evening, an episode of the American radio drama anthology series, The Mercury Theatre, aired over the Columbia Broadcasting System radio network, and brought the idea that there might be life on Mars back into public consciousness. Directed and narrated by actor and future filmmaker Orson Welles, the episode was an adaptation of H. G. Wells' novel *The War of the Worlds* (1898). The radio drama's use of news-like presentation in its version became famous for allegedly causing mass panic, although the scale of the panic is disputed as the program had relatively few listeners.

In 1960, Cornell University astronomer Frank Drake performed the first modern, academically approved SETI experiment, named "Project Ozma", after the Queen of Oz in L. Frank Baum's fantasy books. Drake used a radio telescope 26 meters (85 ft) in diameter at Green Bank, West Virginia, to examine the stars Tau Ceti and Epsilon Eridani near the 1.420 gigahertz marker frequency, a region of the radio spectrum dubbed the "water hole" due to its proximity to the hydrogen and hydroxyl radical spectral lines. He reported he found nothing of interest.

Soviet scientists took a strong interest in SETI during the 1960s and performed a number of searches with omni-directional antennas in the hope of picking up powerful radio signals. Soviet astronomer Iosif Shklovsky wrote the pioneering book in the field, *Universe, Life, Intelligence* (1962), which was expanded upon by American astronomer Carl Sagan as the best-selling book *Intelligent Life in the Universe* (1966).

In the chapter that considers the possibility of ancient alien contact, Sagan writes that he was impressed by the fact our ancestors appear every bit as capable as we are to accurately report, record and transmit important information over vast distances in time. If repeated instances of extraterrestrial visitation to Earth happened, we would expect to see many stories of such visits in pre-scientific narratives that describe contact with aliens. And in fact, there are many such stories across many different ancient populations across the planet (to the delight of Ancient Astronaut theorists). Sagan illustrates this hypothesis by citing the 1786 expedition of French explorer Jean-François de Galaup, comte de La Pérouse, who made the earliest European contact with the Tlingit culture.

The contact story was preserved as an oral tradition by the preliterate Tlingit. Over a century after its occurrence it was then recorded by anthropologist George T. Emmons. Although it is framed in a Tlingit cultural and spiritual paradigm, the story remained an accurate telling of the 1786 encounter. According to Sagan, this proved how "under certain circumstances, a brief contact with an alien civilization will be recorded in a re-constructible manner."

He further states that the reconstruction, "will be greatly aided if 1) the account is committed to written record soon after the event; 2) a major change is effected in the contacted society; and 3) no attempt is made by the contacting civilization to disguise its exogenous nature." Additionally, Sagan cited tales of Oannes, a fish-like being attributed with teaching agriculture, mathematics, and the arts to early Sumerians, as deserving closer scrutiny as a possible instance of paleo-contact due to the tale's consistency and detail.

One of the people who took to heart the idea that contact with aliens can be found in recorded history is Zecharia Sitchin. Sitchin (July 11, 1920 – October 9, 2010) was an Azerbaijani-born American author of books proposing an explanation for human origins involving ancient astronauts. Sitchin attributed the creation of the ancient Sumerian culture to the "Anunnaki," which he claims is the story he found when he was able to translate the Sumerian language. The accuracy of his translation is a matter of controversy.

Sumerian is one of the earliest-known written languages. The "proto-literate" period of Sumerian writing spans c. 3300 to 3000 BC. In this period, records are purely logographic, with no linguistic or phonological content. The oldest document of the proto-literate period is the Kish tablet. Records with unambiguously linguistic content, identifiable as Sumerian, are those found at Jemdet Nasr, dating to the 31st or 30th century BC. From about 2600 BC, the logographic symbols were generalized using a wedge-shaped stylus to impress the shapes into wet clay. This archaic cuneiform ("wedge-shaped") mode of writing co-existed with the pre-cuneiform archaic mode. In the same period the large set of logographic signs had been simplified into a logosyllabic script comprising several hundred signs. The pre-Sargonian period of the 26th to 24th centuries BC is called the "Classical Sumerian" stage of the language. Much has been learned, but much more is uncertain.

Sitchin's translation of the Anunnaki tale speaks of a race of extraterrestrials from a planet beyond Neptune called "Nibiru," and how a group of them came to Earth to harvest resources, primarily gold. Using their own genetic material to enhance one group among the many bipedal apes they found on the planet, the visitors created a pliable work force that viewed their "creators" as gods. He found that Sumerian mythology suggests that the planet of Nibiru has an elongated, 3,600-year-long elliptical orbit around the sun. Sitchin also proposed a "planetary collision" hypothesis that superficially resembles one suggested by modern astronomers – the "Giant Impact Hypothesis" of the Moon's formation about 4.5 billion years ago by a body impacting with the newly formed Earth. However, Sitchin's proposed series of rogue planetary collisions differ in both details and timing.

As with Immanuel Velikovsky's earlier "Worlds in Collision" thesis, Sitchin states that he has found evidence of ancient human knowledge of rogue celestial motions in a variety of mythological accounts. In Velikovsky's case, these interplanetary collisions were supposed to have taken place within the span of human existence, whereas for Sitchin, these occurred during the early stages of planetary formation, but entered the mythological account after being passed down via an alien race intentionally seeding the story to humans.

Sitchin's books have sold millions of copies worldwide and have been translated into more than 25 languages, but his ideas have been roundly rejected by mainstream scientists and academics. They accuse him of deliberately peddling pseudo-science and pseudo-history. His work has been criticized for flawed methodology and wrongly translating ancient texts as well as for incorrect astronomical and scientific claims. Despite all this, he remains a legendary figure among today's well-known proponents of the "ancient aliens" theory, who together have expanded Sitchin's work to new levels of public attention. These writers who appear regularly in mass media include Erich von Däniken, Graham Hancock, Giorgio A. Tsoukalos and David Hatcher Childress.

Regardless of how Sumerian civilization arose, it is hard to deny that the myths of the ancient Sumerians predate and inform many of the stories told by the cultures that came after them. For instance, in the Sumerian King List is the first written description of the antediluvian flood. In the Sumerian flood myth, Ziusudra hears of the gods' plan to destroy humanity, and in response he constructed a vessel that delivered him, his family, and the animals from the great waters.

This is reflected in the Genesis mythology of the Hebrew Bible, where Yahweh decides to flood the Earth because of the depth of the sinful state of mankind. Righteous Noah is given instructions to build an ark. When the ark is completed, Noah, his family, and representatives of all the animals of the earth are called upon to enter the ark. When the destructive flood begins, all life outside of the ark perishes.

Make what you will of Sitchin's work of translating ancient Sumerian, further academic consideration should be done to verify or debunk his provocative assertions. Unfortunately, the world's largest collection of Sumerian artifacts was looted in the 2003 Iraq invasion. In the months preceding the war, starting in December 2002, various antiquities experts, including representatives from the American Council for Cultural Policy asked the Pentagon and the UK government to ensure the museum's safety from both combat and looting. Although promises were not made, US forces did avoid bombing the site.

On April 8, 2003, the last of the museum staff left the facilities. Iraqi forces reportedly engaged US forces from within the museum, as well as from the nearby Special Republican Guard compound. Lt. Col. Eric Schwartz of the US third Infantry Division stated that his troops were unable to enter the compound and secure it since they wanted to avoid returning fire at the building. Iraqi forces had built a fortified wall along the western side of the compound allowing concealed movement between the front and rear of the museum. When US military finally entered a week later, sniper positions, discarded ammunition, and 15 Iraqi Army uniforms were discovered in the building.

Unconfirmed reports tell of men in "all-black military outfits" entering the museum and taking specific items in an organized manner while uniformed US forces provided cover outside on April 9. Thefts are confirmed to have taken place between April 10 and 12. When some staff returned to the building and fended off further attempts by looters to enter the museum, the scale of the theft was reported.

US forces officially arrive on April 16. A special team headed by Marine Col. Matthew Bogdanos initiates an investigation on April 21 to quell reports that US forces had looted the museum. His investigation reports that, despite claims to the contrary, "no US forces had looted the building, and there were three separate thefts by three distinct groups over four days." Despite international efforts, few of the stolen artifacts were returned. After being closed for many years while being refurbished, and rarely opened for public viewing, the museum was officially reopened in February 2015.

Besides the Sumerian material, there is strong circumstantial evidence for ancient contact with aliens in the images of flying discs and shield-shaped flying objects recorded in painted art work since prehistoric times. And the Bible's Book of Ezekiel has a description of an object popularly known as "Ezekiel's wheel," famously claimed by some as a UFO sighting report. In the account, Ezekiel describes a "flying chariot" containing "wheels within wheels" and powered by angels...

Ezekiel 1:16

"The appearance of the wheels and their work was like unto the colour of a beryl: and they four had one likeness: and their appearance and their work was as it were a wheel in the middle of a wheel."

Various pieces of artwork have been made depicting this "wheel within a wheel" as a spaceship of some type with each getting more and more fantastical and distant from the actual source description. Authors that have alleged the "ancient aliens" explanation of the book include Joseph Blumrich, who wrote *The Spaceships of Ezekiel* (1974).

Then there is this evocative description of heavenly assistance from the Book of Exodus, "And the LORD went before them by day in a pillar of cloud, to lead them the way; and by night in a pillar of fire, to give them light; that they might go by day and by night."

Lastly consider this historical record from old Europe. A broadsheet news article printed in April 1561 describes a mass sighting of "air ships." The broadsheet, illustrated with a woodcut engraving and text by Hans Glaser, is archived in the prints and drawings collection at the Central Library in Zürich, Switzerland.

According to the broadsheet, around dawn on April 14, 1561, residents of Nuremberg saw what they described as an aerial battle, followed by the appearance of a large black triangular object and then a large crash outside of the city. The broadsheet claims that witnesses observed hundreds of spheres, cylinders and other odd-shaped objects that moved erratically overhead. The report describes objects of various shapes including crosses, globes, two lunar crescents, a black spear and tubular objects from which several smaller, round objects emerged and darted around the sky at dawn.

The first recorded use of the term "flying saucer" for an unidentified flying object was to describe a probable meteor that fell over Texas and Oklahoma on June 17, 1930. Some who saw the weird light described it as a huge comet, a flaming flying saucer, a great red glow, or a ball of fire. The highly publicized sighting by pilot Kenneth Arnold on June 24, 1947, resulted in the popularizing of the term "flying saucer" by US newspapers. Although Arnold never specifically used the term "flying saucer", he was quoted at the time saying the shape of the objects he saw was like a "disc," and that they moved like "saucers skipping across the water."

Right around the time of the Arnold report, William Brazel, a foreman working on the Foster homestead, noticed clusters of debris approximately 30 miles (50 km) north of Roswell, New Mexico. The date was "about three weeks before July 8," is how it appeared in later stories featuring Brazel, but the initial press release issued on July 8 from the Roswell Army Air Field (RAAF) said the find was "sometime last week," suggesting Brazel found the debris in early July.

Brazel told the Roswell *Daily Record* that he and his son saw a "large area of bright wreckage made up of rubber strips, tinfoil, a rather tough paper and sticks." He paid little attention to it but returned on July 4 with his son, wife and daughter to gather up some of the material. Some accounts have described Brazel as having gathered some of the material earlier, rolling it together and stashing it under some brush. The next day, Brazel heard reports about "flying discs" and wondered if that was what he had picked up.

On July 7, Brazel saw Sheriff Wilcox and "whispered kinda confidential like" that he may have found a flying disc. Another account quotes Wilcox as saying Brazel reported the object on July 6. Wilcox called Roswell Army Air Field (RAAF), whereupon Major Jesse Marcel and a "man in plainclothes" accompanied Brazel back to the ranch where more pieces were picked up.

On July 8, 1947, RAAF public information officer Walter Haut issued a press release stating that personnel from the field's 509th Operations Group had recovered a "flying disc," which had crashed on a ranch near Roswell. Reported in the July 9, 1947, edition of the Roswell *Daily Record*, the story went global through the news-wire service. Meanwhile Colonel William H. Blanchard, commanding officer of the 509th, contacted General Roger M. Ramey of the Eighth Air Force in Fort Worth, Texas, and Ramey ordered the object be flown to Fort Worth Army Air Field. The story then changed and Warrant Officer Irving Newton confirmed Ramey's opinion that the object was a weather balloon. Another news release was issued, this time from the Fort Worth base, describing the object as being a "weather balloon."

Years later, the military decided to issue another story about the event. Officially, the weather balloon story was admitted to be a cover-up for the true purpose of the crashed device... a high-altitude descent capsule with test dummies inside (little alien-sized test dummies...).

And why did they have to lie about a high-altitude descent capsule? Well... the Cold War!

Under the watchful gaze of Commanding General Ramey, another press conference was called featuring debris (foil, rubber and wood) said to be from the crashed object, which matched the weather balloon description. Major Jesse Marcel's expression in the press photos have to be seen to be appreciated. The man who told the world the US had captured a flying saucer is now pictured kneeling before tin foil and admitting it was a balloon. Historian Robert Goldberg wrote that the intended effect was achieved: "the story died the next day."

Subsequently, the incident faded from the attention of UFO enthusiasts for more than 30 years. Interest waned until the late 1970s, when researchers who started calling themselves "ufologists" began promoting a variety of increasingly elaborate theories, claiming that one or more alien spacecraft had crash-landed, and that the extraterrestrial occupants had been recovered by the military, who then engaged in a cover-up to enable it to conduct research on the alien technology in secret.

This story was subsequently boosted by the testimony of Robert Lazar. In May 1989, Lazar appeared in a special interview with investigative reporter George Knapp on the Las Vegas TV station KLAS, under the pseudonym "Dennis" and with his face hidden, to discuss his purported employment at "S-4" (Subsidiary Facility 4), a place that he claimed was part of a United States Air Force secret facility designated "Area 51." At the time the secret test site Area 51 was completely unknown to most of the general public.

Lazar claims to have worked on reverse engineering extraterrestrial technology at S-4, and that the UFOs uses gravity wave propulsion. He said the wave system was powered by an as-yet undiscovered element, one that would have the qualities to be listed as "Element 115." Besides confirming the existence of Area 51, officialdom has denied Lazar ever worked at Los Alamos except as a subcontract technician. There was no way to verify any of Lazar's claims, and the more extreme ones such as having read US government briefing documents that describe alien involvement in human affairs for more than 10,000 years lessened his credibility.

However, when in 2003, a joint team of Russian and American scientists at the Joint Institute for Nuclear Research (JINR) in Dubna, Russia, announced a new chemical element with the atomic number 115 had been successfully synthesized, his name was back on the minds of anyone interested in "ufology." Element 115 was officially named "Moscovium" after the Moscow oblast, where the JINR is located. It turns out element 115 is an extremely radioactive element: even its most stable known isotope, moscovium-290, has a half-life of only 0.8 seconds. Only about 100 atoms of moscovium have been synthesized to date according to reports.

Any review of the UFO phenomenon has to include the people who claim to be "contactees." Contactees are persons who claim to have experienced contact with extraterrestrials. Some claim ongoing encounters, while others claim to have had as few as a single encounter. As a cultural phenomenon, contactees perhaps had their greatest notoriety from the late 1940s to the late 1950s, but individuals continue to make similar claims in the present. In my estimation, most people who have had such experiences tell no one or only shared their story to small groups of intimates. Some have gone public and formed support groups, and a few have spoken publicly at UFO conventions.

The contactee movement has seen some limited attention from academics and mainstream scholars. Among the earliest was the classic 1956 study, *When Prophecy Fails* by Leon Festinger, Henry Riecken, and Stanley Schachter, which analyzed the phenomenon but only focused on the story of a small UFO cult in Chicago called the Seekers that believed in an imminent apocalypse, as well as the group's coping mechanisms after the event did not occur. There have been at least two university-level anthologies of scientific papers regarding the contactee movement.

The most significant research in this area has to be the work done by John Mack. John Edward Mack M.D. (October 4, 1929 – September 27, 2004) was an American psychiatrist, parapsychologist, writer, and professor at Harvard Medical School. He was a Pulitzer Prize-winning biographer, and became the leading academic researcher and writer on alien abduction experiences of his time. He was also a campaigner for the elimination of nuclear weapons.

In the early 1990s, Mack commenced a decade-plus study of 200 men and women who reported recurrent alien-encounter experiences. Such encounters had seen some attention from academic figures such as R. Leo Sprinkle in the 1960s. Mack, however, remains the most esteemed academic to have studied the subject. It is a tribute to his dedication to the truth that he continued his work even when it elicited considerable criticism from his colleagues at Harvard.

He initially suspected that such persons were suffering from mental illness, but when no obvious pathologies were present in the persons he interviewed, his consulted his longtime friend Thomas Kuhn, who predicted that the subject might be controversial, but urged Mack to collect data and ignore prevailing materialist, psychological explanations. Soon, Mack began concerted study and interviews.

Many of those Mack interviewed reported that their encounters had affected the way they regarded the world, including producing a sense of spirituality and an urgent concern for the environment. Consistent themes in the encounters began to emerge.

Mack was clearly aware of the sensitivity of the work he was doing and remained guarded in his interpretation of what soon came to be known as "alien abductions." Professor Terry Matheson, a critic of Mack, writes that "On balance, Mack does present as fair-minded an account as has been encountered to date, at least as these abduction narratives go." In a 1994 interview on the TV show, "Thinking Allowed", the host, psychologist Jeffrey Mishlove, observed that Mack seemed to be "inclined to take these reports at face value." Mack replied by saying, "Face value I wouldn't say. I take them seriously. I don't have a way to account for them." Similarly, on the BBC, Mack says, "I would never say, yes, there are aliens taking people. I would say there is a compelling powerful phenomenon here that I can't account for in any other way, that's mysterious. Yet I can't know what it is but it seems to me that it invites a deeper, further inquiry."

Mack noted that there was a worldwide history of visionary experiences, especially in pre-industrial societies, that psychologically mirrored modern "abduction" experiences. One example is the vision quest common to some Native American cultures. Only fairly recently in Western culture, notes Mack, have such visionary events been interpreted as aberrations or as mental illness. Mack suggested that abduction accounts might best be considered as part of this larger tradition of visionary encounters.

His interest in the spiritual or transformational aspects of people's alien encounters, and his suggestion that the experience of alien contact itself may be more transcendent than physical in nature, yet nonetheless psychologically real, set him apart from many of his contemporaries, such as Budd Hopkins, who advocated the physical reality of aliens.

His later research broadened into the general consideration of the merits of an expanded notion of reality, one which allows for experiences that may not fit the Western materialist paradigm, yet deeply affect people's lives. His second (and final) book on the alien encounter experience, *Passport to the Cosmos: Human Transformation and Alien Encounters* (1999), was as much a philosophical treatise connecting the themes of spirituality and modern worldviews as it was the culmination of his work with the "experiencers," his preferred term, to whom the book is dedicated.

Mack was killed on September 27, 2004 in a hit-and-run at a well-marked London street crossing. Despite London having the highest density of surveillance cameras of any city on Earth, neither the driver nor the car was ever identified.

As a psychologist and an "experiencer" myself, my opinion is that the contactee movement is a rich mine for anthropologists, psychologists, and any sincere scientifically minded individuals who seek to unearth answers to some of life's deepest questions.

The question that John Mack sought to answer remain central to our search for truth in the field of UFOs and extraterrestrials:

Were the contactees in touch with anything other than their own internal fantasies?

Are the experiences actual physical events that the aliens cover up with technology beyond our understanding?

Are they out-of-body experiences that are taken out of context?

All of the above and something else we can't even imagine??

Since the time of Barney and Betty Hill, the American couple who claimed they were abducted by extraterrestrials in a rural portion of New Hampshire in 1961, a whole lot of people have recovered memories of something they can't really explain. The Hills' experience was the first widely publicized report of an alien abduction in the United States, and the incident came to be called the "Zeta Reticuli Incident" because the couple stated they had been kidnapped by aliens who claimed to be from the Zeta Reticuli system. Their story was adapted into the best-selling 1966 book "The Interrupted Journey" and a 1975 television movie "The UFO Incident." In September 2016, plans were announced to make a feature film based on the events.

Most of Betty Hill's notes, tapes, and other items have been placed in the permanent collection at the University of New Hampshire, her alma mater. In a sign of changing public opinion towards claims of alien encounters, in July 2011, the state's Division of Historical Resources marked the site of the alleged first approach of the alien craft towards the Hills' car with a historical marker.

Contactee accounts generally differ from those who allege alien abduction in that contactees usually describe beneficial experiences involving human-like aliens, whereas abductees, as the term they prefer implies, do not recall their experiences as voluntary or cooperative on their part.

George Adamski (17 April 1891 – 23 April 1965) was the prototypical good experience "contactee." A Polish-American citizen who became widely known in ufology circles, and to some degree in popular culture, Adamski claimed to have photographed spaceships from other planets, met with friendly Nordic alien "Space Brothers", and to have taken flights with them to the moon and other planets.

He was the first, and most famous, of the so-called contactees of the 1950s. Adamski called himself a "philosopher, teacher, student and saucer researcher," though most investigators concluded his claims and photos were an elaborate hoax, and that Adamski himself was a con artist. Adamski authored three books describing his meetings with Nordic aliens and his travels with them aboard their spaceships: *Flying Saucers Have Landed* (co-written with Desmond Leslie) in 1953, *Inside the Space Ships* in 1955, and *Flying Saucers Farewell* in 1961. The first two books were both bestsellers. Adamski became wealthy and sold nearly half a million combined copies.

Among the many contactees that spoke out about their experiences in the 1950s, I became draw to the unique story of George Van Tassel...

A short history of George Van Tassel

Van Tassel was born in Jefferson, Ohio, in 1910, and grew up in a fairly prosperous middle-class family. He finished high school in the 10th grade and held a job at the Cleveland airport where he acquired a pilot's license as a teenager. At 20, he headed for California, where at first he worked at a garage owned by an uncle. While working at the garage he befriended Frank Critzer, an eccentric loner who claimed to be working a mine somewhere near Giant Rock, a seven-story boulder near Landers, California. Frank Critzer was a German immigrant who eked out a living mining gold in the desert, and by his own account, the old prospector introduced Van Tassel to the secrets of living in the desert and instilled in him a love of the area.

Van Tassel became an aircraft mechanic and later graduated to flight inspector. At various times between 1930 and 1947, he worked for Douglas Aircraft, Hughes Aircraft, and Lockheed. Van Tassel enjoyed an excellent professional reputation. While at Hughes Aircraft he was named a top flight inspector, and was one of two personal favorite wingmen of Howard Hughes. Hughes was known to occasionally visit Van Tassel by flying into the small airport at Giant Rock that Van Tassel ran after his retirement.

During World War II, Frank Critzer came under suspicion as a German spy and was killed during a police raid of his home at Giant Rock in 1942. Upon receiving news of his old friend Critzer's death, Van Tassel was distraught and looked into acquiring the abandoned airport near Giant Rock from the Bureau of Land Management, who managed the land. He was eventually given a long-term Federal Government contract to develop the airstrip and the land around it. Five years later, at the top of his profession, Van Tassel unexpectedly quit southern California's booming aerospace industry to retire to the abandoned airstrip in the desert in 1947. When Van Tassel and his family arrived at the site, bloodstains from his friend's violent death were still on the walls of the abandoned underground hovel. The carved-out rooms were the only shelter available to the Van Tassel family when they moved onto the property.

Van Tassel and his family at first lived a bare existence in the simple caves Frank Critzer had dug out under Giant Rock. After much work, Van Tassel turned the caves into comfortable rooms, and eventually built a modern style house at the airfield. At the height of their activity, the Van Tassel family ran a café, the airstrip, and a dude ranch beside Giant Rock. His plan for an active yet simple retirement before the age of 40 was coming together. Van Tassel and his family thrived in the desert. Besides running a dude ranch and the main stopover point for weekend aviators in the southern California high desert, Van Tassel spent much of his time in various forms of Christian-inspired deep meditation. His favorite place to meditate was in the deepest room under Giant Rock.

This quiet life changed in 1952 when, Van Tassel claims, he began to receive psychic messages while in a state of deep meditative trance. The messages claimed they were coming from the commanders of extraterrestrial spaceship in orbit above Van Tassel while he was practicing deep meditation under Giant Rock. Overcoming an initial hesitation, Van Tassel entered into long conversations with these voices. These contacts intensified and at one point he was given a message to pass to the US government that a large fleet of their crafts would be doing a fly-by of Washington, DC later in the summer. Van Tassel duly sent a registered letter to the White House. It is unclear if the letter was ever read by anyone who took it seriously.

As the letter predicted, a number of UFOs sightings were reported in mid-July of 1952. In what became known as the Washington, DC, UFO incident (also called the Washington National Airport Sightings, and more fancifully, the Invasion of Washington), the area around the Capitol saw an unprecedented number of UFOs reported from July 12 to July 29, 1952. The most publicized sightings took place on the consecutive weekends of July 19–20 and July 26–27. UFO historian Curtis Peebles said of the incident, "Never before or after did Project Blue Book and the Air Force undergo such a tidal wave of (UFO) reports."

Van Tassel reports one year after the "UFO wave" over Washington, DC, on August 24, 1953, he was invited aboard a UFO piloted by a being called Solganda. For George Van Tassel, everything would now change. He later writes extensively about what he experienced in several books, *Into This World and Out Again: a Modern Proof of the Origin of Humanity* (1956), *The Council of Seven Lights* (1958), and *When Stars Look Down* (1976). In the books, Van Tassel takes a materialistic approach to describing how late one night, the occupant of a spaceship from the planet Venus woke him up, invited him on board the spaceship, and both verbally and telepathically gave him a technique for rejuvenating the human body. I will expand on my interpretation of Van Tassel's claims later, but for now, note that his visitor is from Venus, the planet of feminine energy, rather than the typical home world for interplanetary visitors at the time, Mars.

Inspired by his encounters and continuing telepathic contact with his alien guides, in 1954, Van Tassel and others began building what they called the "Integratron," based on the "new science" he was receiving from the aliens. To perform cellular rejuvenation, according to Van Tassel, the Integratron was supposed to harness energy from the geology of the site and then amplify it through the structure and equipment onsite and create an energy field that would optimize human health from a molecular level. When fully completed, the Integratron was to be a structure for scientific research into the nature of time, anti-gravity and extending human life.

Built partially upon the research of Nikola Tesla and Georges Lakhovsky, Van Tassel described the Integratron as being created to connect scientific and spiritual evolution, and claimed that when it is powered up, the Integratron would be able to recharge and rejuvenate hundreds of people at a time just by having them walk through the "Integration field" for a few minutes. Van Tassel and his team of believers made slow progress and it took years to get the domed superstructure and the strange looking rotating metal apparatus attachment (Van Tassel called them an "electrostatic dirod") completed. Van Tassel worked meticulously to ensure that the entire structure was made non-ferromagnetic. It was constructed using only wood, concrete, glass and fiberglass, avoiding even metal screws or nails.

The Integratron was never fully completed due to Van Tassel's sudden death a few weeks before the official opening of the facility from what was believed to be a massive heart attack. His family was unable to financially support the project after his death and the structure was sold and went through several incarnations including a stint as a desert disco. In recent times, it has been bought by some people who visited the unfinished Integratron and felt rejuvenated just by staying there. It is now available for rent to people who wish to take advantage of the excellent resonant acoustics of the now completed building. It is often used to stage "sound baths" inside.

Van Tassel was very active among the group of well-known 1950s contactees consisting of George Adamski, Truman Bethurum, Orfeo Angelucci and many others. He hosted "The Giant Rock Spacecraft Convention" annually from 1953 to 1978, which in its peak in 1959 attracted as many as 10,000 attendees. Guests trekked to the desert by car or landed airplanes on Van Tassel's small airstrip, grandly called Giant Rock Airport. Every famous contactee appeared personally at these conventions over the years, and many more not-so-famous ones.

Some references often state that the first and most famous contactee, George Adamski, pointedly boycotted these conventions. In fact, Adamski attended the third convention, held in 1955, where he gave a 35-minute lecture and was interviewed by Edward J. Ruppelt, who was once head of the Air Force Project Blue Book. It was, however, the only such convention Adamski ever attended.

Before his sudden and untimely death, Van Tassel founded two metaphysics research organizations called The Ministry of Universal Wisdom and The College of Universal Wisdom to codify the spiritual revelations he was now regularly receiving via communications with "the people from Space." Van Tassel is a largely forgotten figure today even among ufologists. His blend of Biblical and universal religion didn't go down well with more secular researchers. And it is probably also true that his involved depictions of flying around in pointy spaceships with human-looking alien pilots who have names that reminded some of Flash Gordon didn't help his message go any further than it did.

Without being George Van Tassel, it is impossible to know what he experienced. However, even he himself cannot be certain that what he experienced is what he "thinks" he experienced. As far as I can find, Van Tassel never changed his conclusion that his alien encounter experiences happened in physical material reality. His claimed telepathic communications aside, the "aliens" in Van Tassel's experience are physical beings that fly around in physical spacecraft. However, in the light of John Mack's research years later, it is possible to reinterpret Van Tassel's testimony in a new way. To me, it is telling that his initial meeting with his "guide," Solganda, occurred to him as being "awakened from a deep sleep." After the journey to Venus, Van Tassel is returned to sleep in his bed, and remembers the experience as a real physical journey. But it does begin and end with him asleep in bed. He goes on to have many more telepathic experiences and even "invents" the Integratron with the information he obtains from the "aliens."

This sounds like a description of some of the out-of-body experiences that I have had. If I had not already been aware that I was having OBEs, it would have been easy to confuse what was happening. It must be almost impossible for anyone who has never had any experiences that feel so real that they could not tell the difference from "reality" to imagine what I am trying to describe. I can only say that I have had some experiences while in an out-of-body state that were so real that after returning to "normal" consciousness, I remember them as even "more real" than awake in physical reality. The first time I experienced an OBE starting directly from sleep, it happened in a way similar to what Van Tassel described. I remember being asleep and then I heard a voice say loudly, "Awake!" At the same time, I felt pulled upright from the bed by an invisible force. As I open my eyes, I can see that I am standing on my bed, but the bed is now on the stage of a brightly lit auditorium…

If I didn't already know that I could, and indeed had been intentionally trying to have OBEs, my mind might not have been able to realize that this was not a physically real experience at all. In this instance, I was able to quickly react to what happening and realize I was not in physical reality. However, the realization did not come from any lack of reality in what I was being presented. In fact, my first words were, "Wow, it's just like my wife said, it's so real!"

However, I am very cognizant of the fact that no one can exactly experience what others experience. Therefore, I respect Van Tassel's interpretation of his experiences as having taken place in our shared consensus reality, AKA physical material reality. Like Van Tassel, many people also report being given diagrams and plans for advanced technology by guides that they are able to understand while in an out-of-body state, but they are either unable to remember, or remember what, when recall and record are attempted, appears as gibberish upon return to normal consciousness. Van Tassel's lifelong career in advanced aviation could have enabled him to retain the information given to him by Solganda better than the average person, or it could simply be that his mechanical training allowed his subconscious mind to present the plans for the Integratron to his conscious mind as a gift from the "other," when it was really his own invention.

Van Tassel's sudden death also killed the Integratron. The completed building as it stands now is stripped of the electrical equipment and special cladding that Van Tassel had just finished attaching to the outside of the circular wall before he died. Sadly it was the final step in the construction of his dream, but Van Tassel never lived to see it powered up. The way Van Tassel die was somewhat unusual, and as some of his friends recalled, it came right after two men in military uniform visited the café and spoke with Van Tassel for over an hour. Supposedly they asked him to sell the Integratron and the rights to the land it sits on for several times what he paid. Of course, Van Tassel refused, and the men left. George Van Tassel was dead a short while later of a sudden, massive coronary. To those close to him, his death was completely unexpected as he had no family history of heart disease, had a clean bill of health, and was in excellent physical condition. After his death, his family had to sell everything to cover his funeral expenses, and his extensive collection of expensive and rare electrical equipment "disappeared," or at least no one seems to be able to say for certain who took possession of them in the chaos that followed his sudden demise.

Since Van Tassel's time, popular culture has shifted away from nuanced depictions of our cosmic neighbors like the one in the movie "The Day the Earth Stood" (1951). Based on the 1940 science fiction short story "Farewell to the Master," by Harry Bates, the film tells the story of a humanoid alien visitor named Klaatu, who comes to Earth, accompanied by a powerful eight-foot tall robot, Gort, to deliver an important message that will affect the entire human race. In 1995, the film was selected for preservation in the United States National Film Registry as "culturally, historically, or aesthetically significant."

In the collective imagination of the public, the point of view that there are "nice" aliens, so popular in the 1950s, is almost all gone. Now the image that first comes to mind is that of the scary "alien" that will eat your face and kill you. Is this because Hollywood has become dominated by far simpler images of aliens as devouring monsters like that depicted in the film Alien (1979)? The scary image of alien as horror was repeated countless times, and Alien was followed by three sequels, Aliens (1986), Alien 3 (1992), and Alien Resurrection (1997). By popular demand, director Ridley Scott made a prequel series, composed of Prometheus (2012) and Alien: Covenant (2017) where besides the monstrous creature of the film's title, the advanced race of aliens called the "Engineers" is introduced.

* SPOILER ALERT *

The "Engineers" is even scarier than the Alien because the movie creators made the Alien as a bio-weapon to wipe out humanity!

In the current political atmosphere driven by Trump's demonization of "illegal aliens," the word alien itself is now taking on a derogatory meaning. Perhaps that is why the term "Alien Abduction" packs so much emotional power when it is applied to what people project into their experience. But to me, alien is just "what I do not yet know." The word alien has its roots in the Old French word *alien* meaning "strange." The origin is likely from the Latin term *alienus* meaning, "belongs to another land; foreign." As a noun, it simply meant "a stranger."

After serving as a disco, a home, and office space, among other uses, the Integratron was abandoned for many years. It is currently owned by people who have refurbished the superstructure to the way Van Tassel originally envisioned. They have also placed signboards that tell the basic elements of George's life and how the Integratron came to be. From a small trickle of visitors when it was reopened, the Integratron now attracts a few thousand people a year. Most visitors come to take part in various kinds of "sound baths" offered by different practitioners.

A few of years ago, while my wife was visiting her parents in China, I signed up for one of the sound bath programs offered by a genial-looking fellow working out of Los Angeles. There is no licensing for this kind of stuff, so I wasn't sure what to expect, but for $80, and bring you own food and bedding, I wasn't expecting much. The program started with a tour of where it all started, Giant Rock. A short drive from the Integratron compound, the rock stands out from the surrounding desert through its size and isolation. The dugouts are sealed up with concrete now, and there's nothing of what Van Tassel build except the concrete pad he poured for the café and the small house next to it. The runway is rutted and unusable, but it was still easy to see where planes had landed and taken off from during the heyday of the annual UFO conferences that used to take place here. It is also where Van Tassel boarded the Venusian spaceship for the first time.

The guide told us that Giant Rock has always been considered a holy place to all of the surrounding Native American tribes, and they used to gather there at special times of the year to perform magical rituals to help bring balance to nature. The unique nature of the local geology could be seen in the small hill next to Giant Rock. The whole area consists of beds of quartz crystal and the hill is entirely made of rock crystal jutting out of the desert floor. Most people in the group took a piece or two of the abundant crystal rubble as a memento of the visit.

After dinner, the group sat around the bonfire to talk, and it quickly became clear that while on the surface, our gathering seemed very diverse regardless of age, race, gender, or even nationality, almost everyone had been attracted to the Integratron because they were from the "slightly odd" segment of society. Some had come knowing about Van Tassel's story, but many had no idea of the intriguing back story of the Integratron. Most had driven up from Los Angeles for the weekend, and a few had come from much further. An older couple from England chose the Integratron as one of the stops for their tour of "weird America". Their next stop was the famously haunted Winchester House. A few of us had come from Northern California like me, and we got to talking about our "weird" experiences. I kept my contact experiences to myself and let the others talk. As one lady was talking about her experience with ayahuasca among the Indigenous peoples of the Amazon basin, someone called out, "hey look, is that a UFO?"

Everyone turned to see a bright white light coming in our direction from the east. The desert night was very clear and we had perfect visibility of the light as it sped along in a straight line passing over us. It was impossible to judge its height without any reference, but based on my observation of the speed with which it approached us from the horizon, the light was going much too fast for aircraft. As it passed silently overhead, I said to no one in particular, "unless it changes direction, I am going to say satellite." The light continued for another five or six seconds... then it turned around and came back towards us in a descending arc slowing to a near stop. Everyone freezes... Then it came to a full stop. Everyone starts to talk, "Oh wow!" "Do you see that?" "I can't believe it." The light just hangs there...

A minute or so passes...

Someone points their phone at it, and after a few seconds... "This app says it's the star Vega."

People start to get their stuff ready to go inside. Almost time to start the sound bath...

It was like a UFO didn't just change course and park itself above us. On the other hand, nothing really did happen...

There must have been some kind of look on my face because the ayahuasca lady looks at me and whispers as she passes me, "I think that was for you."

Personal Interlude: UFOs and how I stopped worrying about "lost time."

Before I go on, I had better lay out all of my UFO and "alien contact" experiences to keep things from getting confusing. If it is not clear yet, let me state unequivocally that it is my opinion that it is impossible to fit all "Close Encounters" in any single category. Some appear to be purely psychic in nature, happening only in the mind of the person. On the other end, some appear to involve physical contact that results in implants and surgical procedures. I believe some are likely to be misunderstood OBEs, and we must allow that there are aspects of the phenomena that we simply do not (or ontologically cannot) know.

In all sincerity, having turned the matter over a million-plus times in my mind, I have to conclude I have experienced things that have aspects of most, if not all, of those I listed above. Since I now fully accept that our life is actually lived in a virtual reality based on information and only consciousness is fundamental, the barriers between what is physical, emotional, psychical, energetical, and ontological can sometimes get a little thin. In the beginning, the experiences were "real" to me, in the sense that I believed, "I am seeing a real object flying in the sky." Later, the experiences themselves became such that it was impossible to believe that. In the end, with the work of John Mack in mind, the heartfelt stories of George Van Tassel's life, and the Big TOE of Tom Campbell to give it all a functioning framework, I found my own Integratron. I realized all my experiences were about one thing – the meaning that I found in having them.

November 1993. Tokyo, Japan. Close Encounter of the First Kind

I am lying on the grass in Ueno Park with my Korean girlfriend. I have my hands behind my head and she is snuggled up next to me, head on my arm. It's cold but in the sunshine it feels nice. It has been five months since my dad died. On the outside, I appear to be over it. On the inside, everything is different than before and I still don't really know how I am different. My girlfriend is giving me every sign that I am the one. I can see her dream of getting married soon. I look away. I look straight up through my sunglasses. I see something glinting in the sunshine. Is it a silver balloon? The wind is blowing pretty hard and that thing is staying still…

"Hey, do you see that?" I say and point with the arm she is not lying on. It takes a few seconds of me directing her gaze with my arm straight up in the air for her to see it, but she confirms that she sees it too. As soon as she says she sees it, I notice the object begins to rise. As we watch, it goes straight up with no side-to-side motion at all. In less than a few seconds, it rises out of sight, and we are left wondering what we had just seen.

May 1994. Kailua (North Shore), Hawaii. First night, Close Encounter of the Second Kind

My girlfriend and I are on "practice honeymoon." I chose a secluded seaside bed and breakfast in the small town of Kailua well away from the hustle and bustle of Waikiki. I didn't get out of Tokyo just to get stuck around Japanese tourists. We are having a great time, but there is an undercurrent of tension. Maybe I should marry her even though we are so different in some ways…

Our hosts are an elderly couple with a large house next to the beach. They were on the upper floor and our room was on the ground floor next to the pool

and very private. On the first night we are there, we try out the hot tub and the pool. As I am getting ready to take a picture of my girlfriend in her swimsuit, a small bright light passes slowly behind her. It looked like it was maybe less than a hundred feet behind her head. I pull the frame away from her and snap a few shots of the light. It starts to move away, and I think it probably won't even come out on film. A few seconds later, I noticed the light has come back in our direction in a slow curving line like a small prop plane, but unlike a plane there were no running lights or flashing red beacons, just one bright white light. I watch as the light pull away silently, seemingly close enough that I would hear the engine from any kind of aircraft I know of. My girlfriend tries to follow my line of sight. The light darts off back the way it came and disappears before I can say a word. Something tells me not to go into it and just kiss her. I do that.

May 1994. Kailua (North Shore), Hawaii. Fourth night, Close Encounter of the Third Kind

We are tired from the hot days and warm nights. This night, we go to bed early to be ready for a full day of touristy stuff the next day. I drift off to a deep sleep quickly. Around 3:30 in the morning, (can't explain how I know) a blinding light shines in through the small window above the bed. My first thought is police helicopter. Then I notice there is no copter sound. Next thought, grab the camera! I don't remember actually doing that as the next thing I recall doing is standing up on the bed in order to look out the window. As I get up, I see my girlfriend's sleeping face. I am surprised she is not waking up as the light is flooding the whole room. When I finally get on my feet and turn my face to the light, it seems as if at first the window frame, then the whole wall, becomes a part of the light. I feel a strange peace come over me despite the, shall we say, strange circumstance. My last memory is three shining star shapes coming towards me as I am enveloped by pure white light...

The next thing I remember is I open my eyes and the sun is shining. My girlfriend is still sleeping in the same position as I last saw her. I feel completely awake and refreshed unlike most mornings when I first wake up. I recognized the feeling of "missing time." The last time it happened I took two sleeping pills for a transpacific flight and missed all the meals. I didn't feel time passing, but when I got up I felt like hell. This was different. Definitely no sensation or recollection of any time passing from "go into the light" to "rise and shine." But not only no hangover, this feels... good!

At the breakfast portion of our accommodations, our host apologizes, saying, "sorry for all that noise last night. I have no idea what that was. It is usually so quiet around here." My girlfriend looks puzzled, "was there some noise?" As we get ready to go out, I notice the half-used roll of film in my camera is missing. I am annoyed, as in those days, if you take out a half-used roll of film, you would expose and ruin the whole roll. I was certain I did not take it out from the day before. There were some great shots on that roll. Never did figure out where that film went...

The last night there, we caught the first episode of a new show premiering on Hawaii TV stations, a week later than it did on the mainland... It was called the "X-Files." I loved it. The fact that I just had an experience similar to the one depicted in the show was privileged information in my mind. If I was going to tell anyone, it would have been the woman who was there too, but it just didn't feel right...

"Close Encounter of the Fourth kind" (CE4) was not included in the original Hynek's close encounters scale. Hynek's French associate Jacques Vale argued in the Journal of Scientific Exploration that there should be a CE4 that describes "cases when witnesses experienced a transformation of their sense of reality." This was interpreted to include all abduction-type cases and cases where direct communication with aliens is associated with UFO encounters.

In the time that followed my experience in Hawaii, I did not discuss it with anyone and felt no emotional need to do so. It was as if there was a part of me that had already come to terms with what happened, or knew something about it that made me feel comfortable about it. I had a lot more urgent things to think about anyway.

June, 1994. Mount Takao, Japan. Close Encounter of the Fourth kind

As I was getting ready to wind up my tour of duty in Tokyo, my girlfriend and I finally took up my Japanese teacher's longstanding offer to spend a weekend at her cabin on Mount Takao. The 30-mile drive was an easy job, but without my teacher guiding the way, I would never have found the small cabin at the end of a dirt road deep in the woods.

After settling in and enjoying a wonderful dinner of local specialties with my teacher at the hot spring hotel nearby, my girlfriend and I pulled out the tatami mats while my teacher retired to the bedroom. Night in the woods is dark in a way that city dwellers are not used to. During the night, my girlfriend used the restroom and left the light on in case I needed to go later because she had trouble finding her way in the dark when she went. Fortunately, I didn't need to and slept soundly. In the middle of the night, I am startled awake by the old-style fire station-sounding ring of the phone. It keeps ringing even after four... five... six... Well, I am not going to get up since I don't even know where the phone is. Finally, it stops! I happily drift back to sleep...

A little later, I hear the shoji screen from the back entrance slide open and I sit up with a sense of anticipation. No white light? The room is dark, but I can see clearly even though everything is in a dark shade of purple. I watch as three human figures walk quietly, like thieves in the night, into the room. This time I can see the three consist of an Asian woman with shoulder-length hair, and two men with similar length hair. One had dark brown hair, and the taller one was a blond Nordic type. All three wore a kind of single piece tunic that went to the knee. The taller man has a star symbol on his tunic. It has many points...

A great feeling of familiarity and happiness comes over me.

"My friends, it has been so long!" I say as I rise to meet them. I glance down and note that my girlfriend is sound asleep. I can't make out their faces, but I was certain these three were people that I knew well. The woman sends a thought into my mind, "we have come to close the book."

Hearing these words resonate in the emptiness of the night, I feel sad, but the shorter man hastens to add his thought.

"We will leave a detector and it will send us a signal if there is some change." With a quick motion, he waves his hand under my nose. Some kind of substance, not quite liquid and not quite gaseous, goes up my one of my nostrils.

The other man touches my forehead and...

Missing time again!

The next morning I wake up and don't feel happy. Physically, I was fine, and I was able to be pleasant and normal, but something was different. Oddly,

I didn't think much about what happened the night before. It was as if I knew that "chapter" of the experience was over, and I needed to move on. My teacher said it was so strange that the phone rang the night before. In the 40-plus years since she has had the cabin, the phone has never rung once. Her husband had it put in many years before he died in case of emergencies and they never needed it. She thought it was even stranger that whoever called waited so long without hanging up, but when she finally got there, no one spoke up on the line. Still she was glad she got up and turned off the light to the backdoor since when it is left on, the shadows it casts on her window tend to wake her up.

August 1994. Lake Tahoe, California. Close Encounter of the WTF Kind

There is no Close Encounter of the WTF Kind that I know off, but that is what I am calling the one that happened while I was taking an afternoon nap in the guest house of the summer home of the wealthy couple I used to house-sit for in college. They have remained friendly and invited me to visit for a few days since I was back on vacation during my transfer from the Embassy in Tokyo to the Consulate-General in Guangzhou.

After the long drive from San Francisco, I decide to take a nap before dinner. My mind is heavy, as against my better judgment, I got engaged right before I left Tokyo. I have only been asleep for a few moments when I wake up and notice I can't move...

"Sleep paralysis," I think to myself. It takes me a moment to realize something is not right as my eyes feel closed, but I can still see the room clear as day. At that moment I notice a shimmering movement at the doorway. A human figure floats through the door into room. "She" appears to be a female wearing some kind of skin-tight suit with a helmet that seems to meld right into her neck. The whole outfit resembled something out of Power Rangers. Her appearance is distorted and I can partially see through her, but I can still make out a slender yet obviously feminine form in some detail. I feel a tinge of fear and a sense of "otherness" exuding from her as she comes right up to me. As she gets closer, her form fades out of view. Without any preliminaries, foreplay if you will, I feel her hand enter my forehead.

I can feel a slight tingling and a pressure in my brain as she moves her hand around. I can't see her, but I hear breathing and I can sense the nearness of her breasts to my face while she was literally "playing with my head." A sudden and profound sense of indignation and annoyance floods in. "What the fuck!" I think to myself. "You don't just stick your hand into somebody's head like that."

"I can't believe they did all that work and your brain didn't grow any bigger," a female voice resonates in my head. "You have to eat the (something) gel if you want it to work." With that parting phrase, she pulls out and as quickly as she came, floats back out. I "close" my eyes, and drift into an uneasy sleep. When I wake up, I thought it must have been a continuation of my previous close encounters, and the comment about some kind of "gel" that I could eat to help my "brain grow bigger" stayed with me.

The encounter left a bad "taste" in my mind. Before this happened, I had a kind of melancholy over my feeling that my "friends from space," which was how I thought of them back then, were done with me. After this happened, I was glad they were done with me. For many years, I continued to assume that the "floating woman" was part and parcel of my other Close Encounter experiences. Mainly because they all had the same dreamy yet realistic quality that matched no other experiences I have had (up to that point), and they all happened around the same time. Nothing like that would happen again until more than 20 years later in the desert near Giant Rock when I looked at a fast-moving light and said, to no one in particular, "unless it changes direction, I am going to say satellite."

Over two decades passed between that ghostly hand in my head, and my journey to the desert. I had come full circle. A Close Encounter of the First kind. Something inexplicable in the sky that seems to know what you are thinking. I was a UFO enthusiast since junior high. A little Chinese-American Fox Mulder wannabe before there was such a character. After stuff actually happened to me, I could not help but try to read and watch everything I could find. I told very few people about my experiences. Only friends who I knew to be more than "open-minded," and a few family members. I never even considered mentioning it to anyone at work while I was still at the State Department. I knew I had to tell my wife about them before we got married, but I downplayed their effect on me, and in all honesty, confessed that I have no physical evidence of any of it (where is that roll of film!).

She took it in stride. Whatever she really thought, it was not going to derail our plan to get married. Relieved and glad my future wife was not going to be freaked out by my "confession," I decided it was time to "settle down," be a "grown up," and "take life seriously." Part of that decision led to me try my hand at business. For a couple years after I quit the State Department and moved back to San Francisco, I operated a trading company, and would travel to China to negotiate some contracts. Through a business connection, I met an older Chinese-American former Foreign Service officer who was part of the Nixon delegation to open diplomatic relations between the US and the PRC as an Army interpreter. After the army he entered the State Department and then went into private business. I was so impressed with his post-career success and amazing contacts in both the US and China that on some level, I thought I wanted to "just like him." After a time, I came to see the familiar cracks in the façade.

He could never stop chasing for more "success." He had over a million miles on his frequent flier plan, and still he wants to chase after every option to prove he can "do as he likes." Start another family late in life? Why not? Open a new business? Sure! I brought my wife to meet him when I found out we were all in the same city at the same time. He was busy and talking up different projects to see if I would be interested. At one point, I recall he said, "...then I am flying down to Costa Rica to cut down all the trees for Chinese redwood furniture." I looked at him and saw clearly that "being him" was absolutely not I what wanted. I have not had any contacts with him since. I was attracted to environmentalism in college and even made a donation to Green Peace to "Save the Whales" with one of my first paychecks. But as an adult, I saw the economic need for "development," even if sometimes it causes "temporary inconvenience" to some people. I could be talked into a lot of things if there was profit in it for me as an investor. But after that last meeting, I saw the slippery slope for what it was.

At the not so young age of 46, I finally got married to the woman I met on a plane in Beijing almost ten years before that. I lost a lot to time to be with her by not having grown up enough until that much time had passed. A year before we were married, the position of Administrative Assistant to the Spiritual Assembly of the Bahá'ís of San Francisco opened up. I applied and was hired, so I closed the trading company and began working at the Bahá'í Center located downtown in the Mission District. Homelessness in San Francisco is among the highest in the nation, and the area around the Bahá'í Center is one of the hot spots where many pitch their tents under the highway overpass. There were a number of "regulars" who seemed to have "lived" there for a few years.

I was long-aware that mental illness is a contributing factor to chronic homelessness, but working at a location where I was able to observe the homeless on a day-to-day basis, it became clear that it was a main factor. The Bahá'í Center is open to all seekers, and every so often, an obviously mentally disturbed person will come in to ostensibly ask questions about the Faith. I was probably more equipped than the average Administrative Assistant in dealing with mental health issues, so it was never a problem for me to gauge the appropriate response to the particular person. I even "enjoyed" these interactions with people I would otherwise probably never have the chance to talk to, but it was by far, the most challenging and difficult part of the job. Still, I never had a problem dealing with the mentally disturbed people who came our way. Except for one guy

This guy didn't seem crazy at first. He was kind of nice-looking, in fact he reminded me of Christmas card "White Jesus." He asked to come in using broken English, and was calm and polite. Some kind of Euro-backpacker was my first guess. Can't tell the nationality, but seems German. Turns out he was speaking Turkish. I was happy to make time to speak with someone who seemed like a sincere seeker, so I dropped what I was doing and sat with him for a nice chat. The language barrier made it time-consuming to have a conversation, but slowly I got the impression all was not what it seemed. At this point, our custodian happened to walk behind the guy to get something, and I can see an expression of shock and fear come over his face as he glances at the note pad that the guy has been scribbling on ever since we started talking. Our custodian is big guy and kind of imposing and I don't recall ever seeing that look on his face before.

I use the excuse of talking to the custodian and walk around behind the guy. Oh, I see why the look. The guy had been just writing black lines on the pad and the whole page was almost covered over. We managed to get his name, but when it got personal, he got scared and left. The guy's social media posts were easy to find as his name is not very common. A few months before he showed up at our door, he was a college student in Germany posting about his involvement in the Green Party, and doing video tours of the town he lived in.

Over the next few months, I watched helplessly as he slowly, or rapidly depending on the perspective, descended into decrepitude. He lost all his possessions, bit by bit. His weight plummeted, giving him a skeletal look. Sometimes, he would come to the Center again to rage against "your fake God." Apparently he went to all the churches and temples in the downtown area. Despite our attempts to notify relevant authorities, in a city teeming with mentally disturbed homeless people, the message was "as long he isn't hurting anyone, we can't do anything."

From what I could piece together, he was fixated on "finding God," and had left Germany to look for God in America. Whatever was the original cause of his mental state, what I was hearing from him was that he wanted more attention from God. It was about him... not getting the attention he wants... from God.

His story has a happy ending. After not seeing him for a few months, I feared for the worst, but one day, I see his Facebook account was active again. He was back in Germany among friends. His weight had been regained, and his facial hair shaved off. No mention that I could see of his misadventures in America... Talk about "missing time."

After a lifetime devoted to self-indulgence, my billionaire heiress old contact experienced 10 years of "missing time" in a bed of her own making. I experienced what I consider to be a few years of lost time (and money) in pursuit of a dream of becoming a "successful businessman" with "entrepreneurial" credentials. The guy from Germany definitely spent some "missing time" on the streets of San Francisco. For each of us, in our own way, I believe the time spent held lessons that if learned, would then allow for greater evolution. Each situation was about "getting over yourself" in some way.

I have come to realize that, ironically, the more we selfishly spend time focusing on our "pursuit of happiness," building up the importance of the "little self" getting what it wants, the more time is lost for getting to know our "true self." Perhaps the oldest and most consistent spiritual guidance, from just about every philosophy, faith and belief system, is self-transcendence. In the Bahá'í Faith, that eternal advice is restated by Baha'u'llah.

"There is no peace for thee save by renouncing thyself and turning unto Me; for it behooveth thee to glory in My name, not in thine own; to put thy trust in Me and not in thyself, since I desire to be loved alone and above all that is." - *The Hidden Words*

Krishna, Buddha, Christ and Muhammad all urge us to do the same:

"Strive constantly to serve the welfare of the world; by devotion to selfless work one attains the supreme goal of life. Do your work with the welfare of others always in mind." - *Bhagavad-Gita*

"Though one should conquer a thousand times a thousand men in battle, he who conquers his own self, is the greatest of all conquerors." – *Sayings of Buddha*

"And He was saying to them all, If anyone wishes to come after Me, he must deny himself, and take up his cross daily and follow Me. For whoever wishes to save his life will lose it, but whoever loses his life for My sake, he is the one who will save it." - Luke 9: 23-24

"The most excellent struggle is that for the conquest of self." - *The Qu'ran*

The Bahá'í teachings discourage exaltation of the "lower animal self" through indulgence in vices, passions, and mental intrigues while urging all people to seek self-knowledge, to independently look for truth, to explore the things that open up the understanding of the "true self." Baha'u'llah tells us, it is we ourselves who have the inherent power to discern our material and spiritual natures, and we should use it!

"...man should know his own self and recognize that which leadeth unto loftiness or lowliness, glory or abasement, wealth or poverty." - *Tablets of Baha'u'llah*

Baha'u'llah also describes the station that awaits someone who comes to recognize the unity of all human souls...

"He Who is your Lord, the All-Merciful, cherisheth in His heart the desire of beholding the entire human race as one soul and one body. Haste ye to win your share of God's good grace and mercy in this Day that eclipseth all other created Days. How great the felicity that awaiteth the man that forsaketh all he hath in a desire to obtain the things of God! Such a man, We testify, is among God's blessed ones." - *Gleanings from the Writings of Baha'u'llah*

When we do not recognize our true non-physical nature, it is easy to keep repeating behavior that simply will not work. Revenge is a good example. Violence begets violence. Or as the saying goes, "an eye for an eye, 'til we all go blind." Insanity is doing the same thing and expecting a different result, but let's give that materialism one more try...

"The reason why we don't see the source of our problems is that the means by which we try to solve them are the source." - David Bohm

As for my episodes of "real" and not metaphorical lost time that happened during my Close Encounter experiences, I stopped worrying about those a long time ago. In fact, even right after they happened, it was as if a part of me knew all about it. It felt as if I had been let in on the secret, but I promised not to remember until it was time. To everything there is a time...

Turn, Turn, Turn – Pete Seeger

To everything (turn, turn, turn)
There is a season (turn, turn, turn)
And a time to every purpose, under heaven
A time to be born, a time to die
A time to plant, a time to reap
A time to kill, a time to heal
A time to laugh, a time to weep
To everything (turn, turn, turn)

There is a season (turn, turn, turn)
And a time to every purpose, under heaven
A time to build up, a time to break down
A time to dance, a time to mourn
A time to cast away stones, a time to gather stones together
To everything (turn, turn, turn)
There is a season (turn, turn, turn)
And a time to every purpose, under heaven
A time of love, a time of hate
A time of war, a time of peace
A time you may embrace, a time to refrain from embracing
To everything (turn, turn, turn)
There is a season (turn, turn, turn)
And a time to every purpose, under heaven
A time to gain, a time to lose
A time to rend, a time to sew
A time for love, a time for hate
A time for peace, I swear it's not too late

Chapter Three

ALLIES OF HUMANITY AND THE PRIME DIRECTIVE

My UFO experiences and my conclusion that they were not imaginary did not hamper my acceptance of the Bahá'í Faith. In fact, from the beginning, I was impressed that Bahá'u'lláh offered a very clear statement on the question of, "Are we alone?"

"The learned men, that have fixed at several thousand years the life of this earth, have failed, throughout the long period of their observation, to consider either the number or the age of the other planets. Consider, moreover, the manifold divergencies that have resulted from the theories propounded by these men. Know thou that every fixed star hath its own planets, and every planet its own creatures, whose number no man can compute.

Bahá'u'lláh, *Gleanings from the Writings of Bahá'u'lláh*, p. 163

Bahá'u'lláh's statement that every "fixed star hath its own planets" has now been confirmed by astronomers, and I have no doubt his statement that these planets have their "own creatures" will also be proven in the years to come. The nature of these creatures was later clarified by Shoghi Effendi in *Lights of Guidance* (p. 478), where he wrote, "Regarding the passage on p. 163 of the '*Gleanings*'; the creatures which Bahá'u'lláh states to be found in every planet cannot be considered to be necessarily similar or different from human beings on this earth. Bahá'u'lláh does not specifically state whether such creatures are like or unlike us. He simply refers to the fact that there are creatures in every planet. It remains for science to discover one day the exact nature of these creatures."

'Abdu'l-Bahá, writing in *Divine Philosophy*, (p. 114-115), tells us to expect that beings from other planets will be different from us in their "states of consciousness" as well as the "varying quantities" of the elements that go into the composition of their bodies:

"The earth has its inhabitants, the water and the air contain many living beings and all the elements have their nature spirits, then how is it possible to conceive that these stupendous stellar bodies are not inhabited? Verily, they are peopled, but let it be known that the dwellers accord with the elements of their respective spheres. These living beings do not have states of consciousness like unto those who live on the surface of this globe: the power of adaptation and environment moulds their bodies and states of consciousness, just as our bodies and minds are suited to our planet..."

"The components of the sun differ from those of this earth, for there are certain light and life-giving elements radiating from the sun. Exactly the same elements may exist in two bodies, but in varying quantities. For instance, there is fire and air in water, but the allotted measure is small in proportion. They have discovered that there is a great quantity of radium in the sun; the same element is found on the earth, but in a much smaller degree. Beings who inhabit those distant luminous bodies are attuned to the elements that have gone into their composition of their respective spheres."

A confirmation that "creatures" exist on other planets is very far from confirming that aliens have visited this planet, much less a genetically altered group of bipedal apes to create "a new race of men." But if such visits have taken place and are continuing, it stands to reason that the visitors have taken care to conceal their activities from the general public because despite all the tantalizing tales of Close Encounters over the years, "they" never get caught out in the open for all to see. Could this be because there really are some kinds of rules to visiting less-developed species?

In the fictional universe of Star Trek, there is the concept of the Prime Directive (also known as Starfleet General Order number 1). The Directive is a guiding principle of the United Federation of Planets prohibiting the USS *Enterprise* and her crew from interfering with the internal development of alien civilizations. The Prime Directive was imagined as arising from humanity's own awareness of the harm premature contact can have on others once we had become a star-trekking civilization. This conceptual law applies particularly to civilizations that are below a certain threshold of technological, scientific and cultural development. In such cases, the Directive can even prevent the Star Trek crew from using their superior technology when threatened, if doing so would alter the development of the culture.

Since its introduction in the first season of the original Star Trek series, the Prime Directive has served as the focus in numerous episodes exploring this issue. In the real world, the formation of a human federation that will serve as the basis for our conquests of outer space seems more fictional than ever at the moment. Also it is not clear to me that, even if there was such a group as a "Federation of Planets," the concept of the Prime Directive would turn out to be what is deemed the highest good.

In "The Day the Earth Stood Still," the group that sent Klaatu and Gort knew what was best, and they landed their ship right in Washington, DC, to deliver the message. And the message was clear, if we spread our violent, atomic ways into space, they WILL stop us. In all seriousness, some of the most well-documented cases of UFO contact come from military personnel guarding nuclear facilities. A number of these reports have been unclassified and can be independently evaluated. The witnesses in these records tend to have impeccable military records.

In September of 2010, six retired officers and one former non-commissioned officer from the US and UK held a press conference in Washington, DC, to present witness testimonies from more than 120 military personnel concerning numerous instance of infiltration of nuclear weapons sites by UFOs, some as recent as 2003. In several cases, nuclear missiles would malfunction after a disc-shaped object hovered over them. Captain Robert Salas, a former Intercontinental Ballistic Missile (ICBM) launch officer, was one of the men at the press conference and claimed he was on duty during one missile disruption incident at Malmstrom Air Force Base in Montana in 1967.

According to Salas, an object came over the fence and hovered directly over the launch silos. The 10 Minuteman missiles inside the silos shut down without any apparent cause. The same thing happened at another site a week later. An extensive investigation followed and blamed the malfunction on bad wiring.

Salas says at the press conference he believes, "there's a strong interest in our missiles by these objects, wherever they come from. I personally think they're not from planet Earth."

The most senior officer at the press conference was Colonel Charles Halt. Halt witnessed a UFO directing beams of light into RAF Bentwaters airbase near Ipswich, England, from a distance, then heard reports on the radio that the UFO had landed in the nuclear weapons storage area. Halt believes that the security services of both the United States and the United Kingdom deliberately hid the significance of what occurred at RAF Bentwaters then subverted the investigation that followed.

Of course everyone involved was ordered to never discuss it, but the men said they are sick and tired of the military lying about the national security implications of UFOs at nuclear bases. Robert Hastings, a long-time UFO researcher, who collated the sworn affidavits detailing these experiences for release, lamented that many of the reports of the incidents were only picked up by UFO-themed publications, and never reached the general public. And even if they did, would these accounts make people change their minds?

So, are aliens concerned that we will blow ourselves up, and so will intervene forcefully to stop us from our childish folly, like adults taking matches away from a child? If that is the case, though governments and the military-minded might disagree, couldn't we consider them allies of all humanity? And perhaps it is also true that there a kind of "Prime Directive" that prevents them from openly intervening in such a way that their presence can no longer be denied?

Well, there are about a dozen websites that claim to represent various galactic representatives if you want to hear what they think. Or take the "blue pill" back to the safety of mainstream media, which will tell you that it is all conspiracy theorists trying to sell more books. From what I know now, I would say that Shakespeare was right when he used the title character in the play "Hamlet" to suggest that human knowledge is rather limited: "There are more things in heaven and Earth, Horatio... Than are dreamt of in your philosophy."

My Close Encounters seem rather tame compared to some of the stories told by people who recall visitations that include sexual contact, medical procedures, removal of fetuses, and in some extreme cases, what they perceive to be torture. Still the experiences forever changed the way I look at the world and the universe around us. In some ways it made me less social. Having experiences that I could not share with most people probably pushed me towards sitting in front of my computer doing "research." On this important subject of human-alien contact, I found that while there is a lot of very interesting material on the subject matter available, it is all highly debatable and there is no conclusive evidence available to the public. Although I strongly suspect, conclusive evidence is plentiful in classified databases.

Until I learned how to use out-of-body travel to obtain more information on the beings that I took to be extraterrestrials of some type, I was of the opinion that they also existed somewhere in physical reality. Somewhere in the back of mind was the thought that perhaps they are in an invisible spaceship watching me right now! Since in my personal experience, the aliens seemed intent on helping me, and by extension, humanity, to evolve, I never feared them. The fact that my visitors have all appeared externally human probably made it easier for me to hold such a view. As I've mentioned, it always felt like I had suppressed memories of the events, and at various times, I attempted to use hypnosis to access the memories. Each time, I proved to be strongly resistant to hypnosis although my conscious attitude was cooperative.

Of course, it is possible to argue that UFO experiences could be a kind of self-hypnosis, and I won't argue one way or the other on this point. In my opinion, UFO experiences are like OBEs in at least one way – It is not about the experiences themselves, it is the meaning that one derives from having them this is important. Still in the summer of 2015, something was building up within me… One day, I was watching Senator Bernie Sanders speak at a rally. He touched upon all the groups that Donald Trump had been disparaging and making fun of on the campaign trail… women, blacks, Hispanics, Muslims, poor people, handicapped people, the list was long…

When he moved on, a sudden emotion of being left out came over me…

I thought to myself, "People like me (alien experiencers)" will never be accepted. Even my wife doesn't get it, she just humors me…" Tears welled up and I was caught by surprise at the depth of the feeling. At that moment, my wife walked out of the bedroom and I quickly wiped my eyes. She didn't notice, but I was still a little embarrassed. I quickly forgot about the moment. But maybe someone was listening…

Personal Interlude: My wife was visited by aliens and I slept through it

Immediately after my little inner tantrum about being left out of Bernie's list of recognized "oppressed" peoples, I had totally forgotten about that train of thought. Then later that same night something unusual happened…

Normally, I would get up and drink some water or use the bathroom, but that night, I slept so soundly, it felt like I never moved. I slept without any dreams that I could recall. I don't even remember turning over in bed. But it felt like a normal full night's sleep.

The next morning, as usual, I got up, a little groggy, before my wife, and quietly went about my morning routine. As I sat at my desk without my cup of tea, checking the news, my wife comes bursting out of the bedroom, "They are real, they are really real! I thought you just imagined it, but they are real!!"

Here is her story as it tumbled out of her that morning:

During the middle of the night, she is awakened by a light shining through the "blackout" curtains that we have over the large window in our bedroom. She sees me asleep next to her, but before she can think to wake me, the light becomes so bright, it leaves her speechless. The light somehow starts to dissolve the wall and part of the roof. Now she can see outside into the street and looking up, she sees a barrel-shaped object hovering silently just a little above the houses on our street. There is a band of lights dotting the middle of the barrel and it seems to be slowly rotating. Four small figures start to float down from the barrel and into our room as if they are being transported by the beam of light. My wife is frozen in awe.

The figures walk around the bed to the doorway and stand there as if discussing something. The unbidden thought that these beings are completely not of this Earth, more "alien" than an insect or a worm, pops into her mind. As she has time to look closely at them, she notices that they have some sort of matching uniform. The three smaller ones stood about three feet tall, while the fourth was about a foot taller. Their skin looked rough, almost like bark on a tree, they had faces, but they were "abnormally" thin. Before she could think to do anything, they stopped their "talking" and looked right at my wife. The tall one takes a small cylinder from his belt and as he points it at her, my wife says she starts to hear an "indescribable" sound. The sound gets louder and she goes into total unconsciousness. When she regains consciousness, it's morning, and she knows for a fact, "they" are real.

If I had not had my experiences, I am sure I would probably tell her... a very real dream. As it is, after she tells me the story, I raise my arms to the sky and, and exclaim, "Now, you get it!"

A couple weeks after this breakthrough in our relationship, (she finally gets it!) I notice a draft in our bedroom. Upon investigating, I find the seal between the bedroom window and the frame was all dried up and cracked. In places, the crack was big enough that I could see light come through. I call my handyman and we compared the seal to the window in my office which was put in at the same time. The sealing material of the office window looked much newer and had no cracks in it. Fortunately caulking it fixed the problem.

For weeks after her Close Encounter of the Third Kind, my wife was engrossed with catching up on UFO lore which used to bore her to tears. Like me, after doing her due diligence, she realized that while the evidence for the "ancient alien theory" won't stand up in court, there is a lot of it. By chance, while searching for content for her to watch, I found a video of Tom Campbell talking about how UFOs can sometimes be the way the "Greater Consciousness System" gives someone a nudge to help them realize this is a "virtual reality." OK, you got my attention...

From Tom's material, I found a mental framework for every unexplained event that had happened to us. My wife and I both felt an intuitive attraction to Tom's "Theory of Everything." It just "clicked" for us. From everything we were discovering and experiencing ourselves, it became clear that anyone can have a transcendent experience (sometimes ready, sometimes not). It's a human potential that everyone possesses. Through Tom, I found Bob Monroe's books. Through Bob's books, I learned that binaural sound, particularly in the Theta range, can open the door to OBEs.

I had started listening to binaural sound many years ago after reading about its benefits in harmonizing the two hemispheres of the brain. I would listen when I went on long walks and at night to help me sleep better. I found the effect was subtle, but I liked it. However, binaural's inducing ability or at least that it makes it easier to have OBEs was news to me, and I have never had anything like the intense almost electric vibrations that Bob Monroe describes as an unexpected side effect of his binaural experiments. I soon found a version of the type of frequencies Bob was working with when he started having OBEs from listening to them... The difference from the more musical tones I had listened to before was very noticeable. Soon, I started to notice of feelings of tingling when I closed my eyes. The tingling got stronger, a lot stronger... I had no worries as I had Bob's experiences for reference. I felt I was ready to undertake an intentional attempt to have an OBE.

Most stories of the first time someone comes out-of-body, unintentionally like Bob Monroe, or intentionally, it is usually described as full of hesitation and a little fear. Even people who have prepared well in advance tend to just walk around the room their body is in and look around the area a little. I had a different experience...

Perhaps it was years of regularly listening to "recreational" binaural tones that helped propel my OBEs to a higher level once I found the "medicinal" grade. Or perhaps, it was my strong intent before I made that first attempt, but I honestly did not expect much to happen. I remember thinking if anything did happen, and I got out-of-body, I should see myself on the bed, like what Bob Monroe saw his first time...

In the focus of my mind, I held the thought that if by chance I actually can "travel" and go places once out, I would "aim" for wherever the "head poker" (the ghostly figure who messed with my head in Lake Tahoe some two decades ago) was right now.

The night before I go for it, I grandly announce to my wife that I going to try to go "out-of-body."

She says, "Yeah... sure."

OBE: Looking for someone I don't know

I knew that my first target had to be to verify my UFO experiences. I had long been convinced that these were not fantasies or hallucinations, but were they "real" in the sense that I could find them again? I determined my first attempt would be "her," the head poker It had bothered me for years that the "nice" aliens were more physical-seeming than the one that stuck her hand in my head. Why was she different? Was she even human? Where did she come from?

I had mostly resigned myself to the fact that these questions were never going to be answered. When it occurred to me that OBE or "astral travel" for the traditionalists, just might give me some answers, my intention was set. Tom says in OBE, you just need a clear intent. You don't have to have an address, a direction, or even any idea of where the person you are looking for is right now. Just an identity that you can hold as an intention in your mind to go to...

I lie in bed and relax. I have to admit that I still hold a kind of grudge against the "person" who stuck her hand in my head. The power disparity just felt too great to tolerate. Now I saw a way to find out something about her. I start to through all the things I have learned about OBEs... The rollover technique... The pull on a rope technique... breathing technique... Fear tests... Guardian figures... the silver thread...

Too much to think about, I am just going to use my own technique!

I go through the "Inner Sun" routine… It's not working… I can still feel the bed… Then I start to see an outline of my body lying on the bed. This is new! Everything else is just dark, but I can make out my body, viewed from the POV of me lying in bed, a lighter bit of blue compared to the darkness all around. It did not occur to me at the time, but the image was similar the one depicting Neo's view of the "real" matrix. Instead on seeing lines of green code outlining things, I was seeing my body as blue currents of electric pulses. Oh yeah, this is new…

I try to relax and not think any thoughts or disturb my observation with an emotion. I just wait. Slowly I can see black threads… no… thicker than thread, more like thin electric wire, start to emerge from my "blue energy" body. There is no sensation of them coming out of my body, but I don't feel the bed either… There are a lot of them and they start to wiggle as they make their way up into the air.

"Honey, there are these black worms coming out of my body." I don't feel my mouth, but I can hear the words come out. There is no response.

"What are these things?" I say to no one in particular.

"They are called fasteners." The voice was androgynous. It was on both sides of my head.

"Are they alive?"

"No."

Then all of a sudden, my point of view changes… With no effort at all, I leap up out of my bed with tremendous force and I am flying up at great speed. For a moment as I fly away I glance back and see a dark figure with a square head. It was the size of a house, and it looked like it had been hovering over my bed waiting for me to come out, but I fly away with such speed I barely had time to register it was there. I flew in darkness and had no idea of the direction or the distance I flew, but I held tight to my intention… As I flew, somehow I knew this was still Earth, and in the present moment. For a split second, I think of my body lying in bed, but I catch myself and direct all my attention back to my intended destination…

Soon I could see I was slowing down and entering a dark underground space. I could see the rocky surface and I distinctly noticed how clearly I could see each crack and crevice as I floated over what appeared to be a large tunnel. Ahead I could see a light and I began to slow down even more. There was an opening leading to what looked like a... tree-lined mall of some kind. I see a young woman playing with a group of children near the opening, kindergarten age I would say.

It's her...

She's solid this time and no helmet, and though I never saw her face the first time, I can tell, it's her. I can make out her features just enough to see that she looks... African... Caribbean maybe... I continue to slow... Suddenly, I realized, I am not solid. With that realization, I start to slow to a halt, and as I did, it was as if my body flowed into solidity. In that few seconds, I could see her turn to look in my direction.

"They are going to be able to see me!" The idea was somehow alarming. And with that thought I felt myself drawn backwards at a velocity that far exceeded the one that got me there. There was no sensation of going back into my body, but there was a feeling of falling into sleep. The next thing I know, I was waking up, and it was the next morning.

I was so excited to tell my wife all about it. She listened. She gave her thoughts that it could be a lucid dream type situation. I didn't "really" go to some underground place and see some people. While it might be meaningful, it was in your head, not real people, not a real place, not real experience.

Hum... it was just like with the UFOs... again.

Then I remembered what Sadhguru, the South Indian Mystic, said about truth...

"Something is only true for you if you experience it, otherwise you just chose to believe or not believe."

I am sure if the positions were reversed, I would be the one trying to "talk some sense into her." As it was, I didn't belabor the point, and just went about trying to replicate the experience. And it proved to be as easy as the first time. Without going into every OBE I had after the amazing first time (beginner's luck played a role), I will cover some of the more significant ones.

As you might expect, I tried to find "her" again. However, this time as soon as I come out and ascend into the sky with the intent of finding out more, I see a mass of hooded figures floating above me. Their hoods resemble a bird's head and there must be thousands of them as they blot out my view of the skies beyond with the orderly rows of their ranks.

Perhaps it was because I was "unfastened," but I found being in the non-physical was even more liberating than I expected. I seemed to know how to do things, like flying, by just intuitively knowing... Confronted with this blockade, I "knew" I could blast energy out of my hands at them. With an invocation phrase I recalled from a childhood kungfu story, I extend my palms... "Ru Lai Buddha Palm!" Two powerful beams of light shoot out in a continuous stream. The hooded beings split their ranks to evade and a wide path opens before me. I can't see any of their faces as I fly pass, but I sense that I just scared the heck out of them. However, I lost focus after this encounter and just flew around.

On succeeding nights, I eagerly "exit" my body and fly out into the darkness. However, I found no matter how hard I "intended," I could not get back to that opening. I could sense it was because they did see me... and they closed the door... I try again and again, but just end up flying in the dark. Finally, one night as I am about to give up on my intention of finding "her" again, I am drawn to a figure flying ahead of me in the darkness. Oh, it's her! I give chase. She darts down into a narrow canyon. I give chase. She picks up speed and goes deeper into the ravines. I give chase. Through a crack in the bottom of a large ravine, she slips into what looks like another... dimension?

Of course, I dive in after her.

When I fly pass the bottom of the ravine, the "ground" suddenly twists in a sideways direction. Now we are in a tilted world...

What was the ground was now a wall of rock. She is now falling and jumping from rock to rock. I follow her example, but the gravity is... irregular. I can't keep up in this new rule set that she is obviously familiar with, and she starts to pull away. I see her entering a dark cave in the far distance. There are some deep black figures outside guarding the entrance.

I come to a stop some distance away, but the guards still seem to "sense" me. These guys are wearing tight black leather bodysuits (they look more like black oil) and black motorcycle helmets (no visor) that blend into their necks. They appear to be covered in... no, more like they are… made from black oil. And they look… tough. They start moving forward and it looks like they are sniffing the air. It comes into my mind that if I look away from them, they won't be able to detect me, so I start to look away. As I turn my head to the left, I see a bunch of classic "Dawn of the Dead"-looking zombies with rotting limbs and gore dripping coming towards me. I notice the "black-oil guards" sense them too and seemed disgusted (hard to tell with no face to see, but they mimed disgust with their bodies), and they quickly retreated back to the entrance of the cave.

As more zombies come, I turn my full attention to them, but the first ones are already on top of me…. There was never any fear as I knew this was all happening in the non-physical, so if they "eat" me, so what? More zombies come and they are climbing over each other to get at me. There isn't any biting or grabbing, they just pile on top of me until I can't see anything. It goes black.

I wait patiently to see what happens next. After what seems like about 20 seconds, they start to pile off. Hey, they are (kinda) alive again! They don't seem to even notice me, but are drawn to a light that now appears to my left. Still Looking dazed and confused (like some of the drug addicts I used to see downtown), they walk towards the light. It only takes a minute for the whole lot of them to make their way out… stage left.

The light gets stronger, becoming the light of dawn, and at a little distance to my right, I see more "dead people," but these weren't like the zombies, they looked like classic movie "ghosts." You know, like normal people, but half-transparent. In the front was an interracial couple, arm in arm, the black husband points to the light, and smiling, they walk forwards. Behind them I could see dotting the hills, more people, going towards the light… It's tiring bringing zombies back to life… I am going to fall asleep right there… in the non-physical… Can I do that?

The next day it is an unusually sunny day in what would normally be a time for fog in San Francisco. I feel exceptionally good. I decide to give up trying to find out any more about the "black girl." It wasn't that I was afraid to chase after her, rather I respected that she did not want me to.

I started to experiment with allowing myself to have "no intention," and just let the OBEs happen by themselves…

Soon, I experienced what felt like past lives. In the first one I begin from the point of view of inside a body while it is in a bare-knuckle boxing match... I can feel my arms pumping, feet shifting, but I am not controlling the movement. The vision "zooms" out... and I see the body is that of a tall black man. He is pummeling the other fighter. I "zoom" back in and out again a few more times... Looks like he - "I" - am going to win...

The next time I experience something like this, it is more tragic... It begins with me "waking" to find myself in the body of a man frantically running on a dockside road across from some buildings that I recognize to be 1930s-style China... "I" am running for my life when suddenly a Japanese plane flashes out from above the row of buildings to my right and I see it drop a bomb onto the building next to me... There is an explosion that evaporates the building and destroys the two on either side of it, and I am blasted into the water... I am going down... I can't swim... Now I am not in the body and see it sinking down to the bottom of the dark waters...

...then I am back in a body and feel "myself" pop up to the surface. The feeling of taking that first breath after "drowning" felt so vivid, I almost woke up into the physical right then... But I managed to stay a moment longer and as I drifted out of the person that was now swimming towards the far shore, I could see that it was not an earthly place, but a magical one... Then I realized "I" died in that river...

The last time I went into something that felt like a past life, it strangely entangled into one of my wife's OBEs. My experience saw me "wake" in the middle of an emotional family drama. I was the younger of two Indian brothers. My older brother is trying to persuade me not to leave home. I am insistent and even as he talks, I am packing my bag and checking to make sure I have my passport, I even check the picture and name...

As I prepare to leave, he grabs my arm and looks me in the eye. "You will always have a home here."

I feel a powerful mix of emotions, it is something involving competing with him for something or someone where only one of us can win... so I will go... but I am unable to verbalize it. The experience ends with me walking away...

Experiencing these three snippets of what felt like peeking into another life that at once seemed familiar and alien, made me feel more... whole. Even as I write this, I can't explain how having the experience produced this feeling. But like so much of what I have experienced since learning go "out of body," I did not waste my time of trying to determine "what" the experiences was or how "true" it was in relation to external events. What I focused on was how it was changing who I was on the "being level" to have had these experiences. Tom Campbell drums this point home in his books and talks over and over. You can't "prove" OBEs are "real," but you also can't avoid changing who you are if you experience something like that yourself.

Around the same time, my wife tells me about one of her more unusual OBEs, where the two of us are visiting a tea shop together and it was because the owner of the shop looked so much like a Hong Kong singer that she found it so memorable. We didn't think much of this particular OBE since, by this time, she was having them twice a day, more on weekends (slight exaggeration).

Sometime later we randomly decide to visit a tea shop on a street we shop at often. Before this we had always giving this place a pass as it seemed like a tourist trap and we already have a lot of good tea, but this day, we had some time to walk around before an appointment and thought why not give it a chance. There is a middle-aged Indian guy at the tea table talking to the owner and tasting some tea. I see two people that look like his wife and teenage daughter looking around the shop. We look around too. It is soon clear, the two ladies have been ready to leave for some time and have already looked at everything. The guy keeps talking...

I walk over and ask what kind of tea they are drinking. They invite me to sit down to the obvious exasperation of the two women. My wife sits down and looks at the owner then whispers to me, "He looks like that guy in my OBE, that tea shop owner!"

The Indian man turns to me and instead of tea starts talking about meditation. It was a continuation of what he and the shop owner had been talking about, I assume... How important it was to always make time for 20 minutes of meditation every day... If you feel you have no time, then do 40 minutes of meditation… At this point, his wife says firmly, "we are going to walk around outside". The man finishes his cup of tea and with a smile walks out…

He didn't look anything like the older brother I saw in my OBE, but even in our momentary interaction, he reminded me of the, "I know better than you what is good for you" vibe that I recall not liking…

But my "brother" was right about the meditation thing…

I won't go into some of the more personal experiences that involved me meeting the "Cosmic Buddha" and flying into his head to meditate, or the one with the seventy feet tall Jesus, but let's just say, I was very glad I had "Tom's Three Rules" to OBEs to guide me…

1. FEAR WILL MAKE IT BAD EVEN IF IT ISN'T
2. YOUR BELIEFS WILL TRAP YOU
3. YOUR EGO WILL LIMIT WHAT YOU CAN SEE

It was reassuring to know and accept that what we perceive while out-of-body is metaphorical. Any seeming entanglement with my "real" life I could live with easily as a synchronous event or even toy with the idea that all the experiences are "face value" real. I had my own integrated method and Tom's three rules to guide me in my OBEs. I thought I was really good at this. I did not notice the ego inflation that went with this line of thinking at first…

After hearing me talk about my "amazing" experiences for a few weeks, my wife couldn't take it anymore. She was going to "prove" that just intending didn't get you to a new level of consciousness or create a new type of experience. If anything happened, it would still be like a lucid dream.

So… she starts to listen to some of the binaural tracks that I like… After a bit of this, she lies down one night intending to come out of her body… The next morning, she comes bursting out of the bedroom, "Oh, my leg came out of my body! But this dark shape scared me back in."

Yeah, just like the UFO thing… again.

Since then it has been the story of the tortoise and the hare. And I am the hare.

Once she proved to herself that OBE is another category of experience altogether, another state of consciousness, she threw herself into it. Literally everyday single day since then, she has made time to meditate – usually a few hours at a time. I… don't do that (despite my Indian "brother" telling me to).

I still continued to have many incredible experiences while out-of-body, but I started to lose the enthusiasm of the first couple months, while my wife, being the "tortoise," spent quite a bit of time traveling in our shared consensus reality, i.e. physical world, to confirm her experiences. After she correctly read the four-digit address of her friend's new house, she amazed her friend and further convinced herself what she saw was "real."

I never felt much need to prove my out-of-body experiences were "real." My aim was to go places I could not go in the physical realm, to see things that can't be known in material reality. One night, with the intention of seeing the future of the planet, I find myself outside a large walled compound. It looks much larger than a sports dome, and I can not see around it. A group of very tall beings hooded and shrouded in some kind of dark shimmering cloth stand guard. As I approach them, one move to block me. I look at their faces and realize my mind could not interpret what I am seeing. The area where there would be a face is an image that looks like a shifting kaleidoscope. I sense these beings hold immense power and do not try to push forward and they also do not bother me besides blocking my way. Then an even taller being cloaked similarly, but with an insignia on his right shoulder, come and look at me. His "face" is the same as the others.

After a moment, he says, "You can let this one pass." His voice is… mechanical.

The others move away, and with a nod, I enter the walls. Inside, I see a huge train terminal and other massive transport facilities. Many people are arriving and being directed in an orderly fashion towards what look like the entrances to underground bunkers. There is a sense of tension in the air. I look up and I see why – a huge comet with a tail that stretched across half the sky. I knew the comet was going to hit… soon.

"Is this Earth," I asked no one in particular.

"Yes," said the familiar androgynous voice.

"Is this our Earth?"

"No."

"What year is it?"

"2029."

Following a few weeks of somewhat random "flying around" and passively witnessing various events like the one described above, I found myself being "sent to school" whenever I went out-of-body. Whatever my intent, I would appear at a school setting, sometimes even in school uniform. It was as if I couldn't go anywhere else. I confess I got a little frustrated. I didn't really enjoy school in the physical realm and I didn't like it much in the non-physical either. I sucked it up and taking a cue from my wife, I did a couple months of that.

Then I had a new experience. From a deep sleep, I am snapped awake by a voice saying loudly in my left ear, "AWAKE."

As I open my eyes, I feel my body lift up, not by anything in particular, but as if I am being poured out of the bed. Now I am standing up on my bed. I am still in my pajamas... but I and the bed are in a big white lecture hall. The bed is on the stage and a man (the one who woke me?) to my right wearing a lab coat makes little gestures of presenting me to the "class." Now I notice there are a lot of people there sitting on tiered rows of seats and there is an old 1950s-style TV camera... Everything has this quality of... ultra-realness... I can't help but look at my own hands and marvel, "Wow, it's just like Cathy said, it's so real!"

"Tell us...," the man says, "about the trajectory of love."

"Oh... Well, see... there are these individual particles and they become entangled, but because they only travel at 99.9999 percent of the speed of light, they get twisted into a spiral..." I forget what I was saying... but I am waving my hands around a lot... I keep talking until a teaching assistant, who is sitting on the floor against the wall since there are no more seats, takes his head into his hands and says loudly, "...but that means... IT'S ALL A CYCLE."

"That's it exactly! You've got it!" I finish with a little flourish and jump off the bed. A crowd of people rush over to congratulate me... I pick out one familiar face walking from behind the big TV camera... I don't know who it is (but I know he's Japanese-American), and I say to him, "so you are press now? I guess you can say whatever you want." We smile at each other, then I am mobbed by the crowd and I drift away and back to a pleasant sleep. This was the first OBE I had where that quality of "more real than real" was present. I had read about it, and my wife talked about it, but now I know it is real because I experienced it.

After that I was free to travel again instead of always coming out and landing in "school." One day, while resting on the sofa in my living room, I experimented with trying to go out-of-body outside of my normal situation. No binaural preparation, no meditation, just intention, go.

Starting with body relaxation and moving to breath control, I slowly let go of all sensations from the body. When I felt myself getting lighter as if being lifted from the sofa, I knew it was working. Soon, I found myself in a white hallway, looking into various rooms where people were in class learning various things. What, school… again? I see a man in a white "space suit" down the hall and I yell over at him, "I know all this stuff. I want to learn something new."

After the words come out of my month, I instantly find myself back on the sofa, awake. Well, that won't work, I think to myself. However, just as I finish the thought, the ceiling over me cracks open, and writhing black snake-like forms of all sizes emerge. Some are as thin as a thread and the largest are like an oil pipeline. The thicker ones have moving little legs along the side like a millipede. I gasp out loud.

"Are these alive?" I ask no one in particular.

"No," the familiar voice was more female.

"What are they?"

"Fasteners of Creation," the voice whispered.

Although the words were said quietly, they resonated in my mind. A second later, I "truly" wake up.

So… this is what my wife keeps talking about when she said she has these experiences that are just like those in the movie "Inception," a dream within a dream. I had never experienced anything like this before and so didn't really believe her and instead thought to myself, "I would know if I was still not really awake…" See the pattern of how everyone does that? Not your experience, not your truth. You can only believe or not believe. Belief is not truth.

Now, waking up into a dream, is something that is true for me. I really thought I "was" awake until the ceiling cracked open. Fortunately, I was not afraid and did not turn the experience into a "bad" one even when it wasn't bad or even scary (maybe a little). Later, I found a tiny spinning top I had lying around and, like in "Inception," I spun it to make sure I was not still in a dream (in a dream, it would spin forever). I spun it too hard and flipped it off the table.

OBE: Recovered memories of a higher self

After that I was able to maintain more control of my OBEs. I soon latched onto the intention to see the three "nice" aliens, and learn more about them. With practiced ease, I was able to relive both encounters and obtain more details past the point where my memories used to end with "lost time."

In the first encounter in Hawaii, I was able to see that some sort of "work" was done on me by the three visitors. None of it seemed painful, but some quite intrusive. I got the impression that the "niceness" I perceived before was more because I chose to block out the memory of much of what took place.

When I relived the second visit, I could see that the three seemed very business-like. My affection for them appeared very one way. And I saw clearly the insertion of an implant by one of the men. What I remembered as a kind of liquid smoke was in fact a small filament. Past the point where my memory had faded out before, I could now see the three of them stand over my sleeping form watching silently for some time...

At this point, a physical sensation intrudes and I have to scratch my nose. Oh, can't move... can't see either. The itch that woke me up is now working its way out of my nose. I can feel something wiggle over my face a bit, and then it seems to lift off. A cat hair caught on my breath? Now, I can move and I rub my face. No trace of anything...

But I get an intermittent nose bleed for a few days after this "dream."

For no particular reason that I could consciously relate it to, soon after this dream I began to enter a period of mild depression. As a psychologist, I recognized the signs, and I diligently looked for the cause. I was not too concerned as the mildness of the depression limited its effects on my day-to-day life, but I lost all interest in having OBEs.

It was especially during this time that the tortoise-and-hare quality of my wife's and my different approaches became evident. My wife's consistency in doing meditation paid off in her having many more OBEs than I did. She also had guides who would offer her advice. I, on the other hand, tended to bound from one dramatic experience to another, and besides "school" and the voice that would answers my questions sometimes, I did not have a "guiding spirit."

Intellectually, I tell myself, you should keep up the meditation practice and consistently intend to have OBEs, but emotionally, I just didn't want to... Perhaps, I was just bored of it? No, it was something else... Something that I am not seeing... What am I missing?

The answer came in a way I did not expect. One night, I tried to go out-of-body again, not from wanting to, but more from wanting to keep up with my wife. As I lay there, I just could not get into it. My thoughts wandered around, and suddenly a new experience... recovered memories?

As I lay in the dark, now fully attentive to this new experience, memories came into my mind. Memories of out-of-body experiences that I didn't remember before this moment...

I could tell from the quality of the memory that they were "recent." The images that presented in my mind were not the vivid quality of my OBEs, not the fluid haze that is my fantasies, and not the immersive quality of a dream either. These WERE memories!

At all once, I suddenly remembered how after they detected the change in my mental readiness, the "three nice aliens" returned to visit my "operational self," the part that has these memories, and asked "me" to help out on a "mission." The entirety of the mission itself was absent from the memory playing out... but I remembered it was dangerous... delicate, and ultimately successful.

As the memory unfolds past that part, I see in my mind's eye, the four of us flying away from the place where we had just completed the mission. With a sense of satisfaction, I look back and see we are already high above a dark blue planet, all water and hardly any land… I feel a deep happiness at doing a good job on my first time out with them.

Then I remember the sudden panic. I am the first to sense it because I was looking back and see that someone had just shot at us. I scream in warning, "magic bullet!"

With desperate urgency we increase our speed to maximum, accelerating into wild dives and weaves to avoid this projectile. But it's no good! The thing is much faster and is tracking us!

At this point in the unfolding of the memory, a powerful emotional component takes over the flow of the images. It's as if time is slowed down even in the remembering of the moment. I can see the bullet closing in and I know I have the power to alter the probability of its trajectory – it is why they chose me! I see the bullet heading towards the first one. I try as hard as I can, I give it everything I have, and the bullet starts to curve… I was making a difference!

But it was too close, no more time – the bullet curves and enters the second one.

He is killed instantly. His body winks out of existence. It's done. There is nothing to do to change it…

Now in the memory, the emotional component is overwhelming. There is a level of rage that I can't recall ever feeling in "real life." There is no time for thought. I turn back to the place where the bullet came from and I intend Utter Destruction upon that place. From the vast distance we had come, we could only see a tiny flash on the face of the planet far below us, but somehow in the memory, I knew… I just nuked that place…

Before there was time for regret, I register the shock on the faces of the remaining two. In an instant, they move far away from me and I can remember the sense of finality in their thoughts being projected at me, "we can no longer work with you."

I lay still in bed… the whole "package" unfolded in what seemed like a split second, and I was fully aware the whole time… definitely new experience…

Now, I get it... No wonder I am depressed. My "higher self" gets a job offer, and first day on the job, "he" blows the crap out of the place they were supposed to help. "The Three" lived what my higher self only thought he understood. It is not about living or dying. Yeah, they can't work with some primitive like me... first thing I do when I get mad is nuke somebody... So human...

Self-Analysis Session 689

Analysand: So, Doctor Yen, what am I to make of that experience? Now there is a "higher self" that's doing something I am not aware of all the time? I suppose "he" was with "me" all along...

Analyst: Well, I suppose you can take comfort in that fact that we can sincerely categorize all of these unusual experiences so far as feeling like it is coming from "God." In the Bahá'í faith, it is accepted that anyone can have extraordinary experiences that defy normal consciousness because as Abdu'l-Baha revealed in *Paris Talks* on page 86, "by the power of the Holy Spirit, working through his soul, man is able to perceive the Divine reality of things."

Analysand: So, even if everything I have described so far was happening only "in my head," these OBEs were experienced as a psychological reality. What happened in them mattered to me and the emotions I felt were as strong, if not even greater than, those felt in physical material reality. Therefore, at a minimum, these experiences can be used for personal growth and evolution.

Analyst: But it is also possible that these experiences are not limited to the personal level.

Analysand: So if we can learn to interact with beings that are not simply a part of our own psyche, we would be able to help the growth and evolution of other beings...

Analyst: Okay, our time is up, we will see you next time.

Chapter Four

THE HUNGRY DEAD

After the "recovered memory" experience, my depression was completely lifted. As a practical psychologist, it didn't matter if the science fiction story that the memory consisted of had any validity in this or some other dimension, the psychological truth was the "patient" felt better. Physician, heal thyself... Yeah, I just did.

Soon, I felt the urge to try for OBEs again. Out of curiosity, I tried to see what my "higher self" was doing. It was kinda funny, but "he" was working at an "energy" processing factory as a mid-level manager. Apparently "he" was more suited to this job and was known for being "nice." And not nuking anyone...

Looking for something meaningful to do, and to see if I could find evidence that the experiences were not just personal, I went all the way back to my first paranormal experience, the ghost girl in Taiwan that my friend and I saw late one night in the middle of "Ghost Month"... Yeah, that's a great idea!

For people who still believe, the time of the Hungry Ghost Festival (Yu Lan 盂蘭) or Ghost Month is the time of year when the gates to the spirit world are opened and the deceased walk the earthly plane again searching for their living relatives, potentially angry, and definitely hungry. Traditionally, it is believed that ghosts haunt the island of Taiwan for the entire seventh lunar month, when the mid-summer Ghost Festival is held. The time is known as Ghost Month in English.

The first day of the lunar month is marked by opening the gate of a temple, symbolizing the gates of hell. On the 12th day, lamps on the main altar are lit. On the 13th day, a procession of lanterns is held. On the 14th day, a parade is held for releasing water lanterns. Incense and food are offered to the spirits to deter them from visiting homes and spirit paper money is also burnt as an offering.

Fourteenth day... That's right around the time we saw her.

During Ghost Month, people who observe this tradition try to avoid surgery, buying cars, swimming, moving house, marrying, even whistling and going out or taking pictures after dark for fear of ghosts forming an attachment. It is also important that addresses are not revealed to the ghosts as they might follow you home that way, or in other words, become "entangled" with you. In places like Hong Kong, China, Taiwan, Thailand, Malaysia, and Japan, the seventh month of the lunar calendar is considered scary by a lot of people. The 15th day of the month is the peak for ghostly activity and culminates with the Hungry Ghost Festival. On this day it is vital to offer sustenance, usually incense and other burnt offerings, but also food and drink, to your dead ancestors – or any other ghosts that might cross your path.

Otherwise they will haunt you, or even worse, curse you.

Haunt you or curse you. Well, no wonder people are scared if that is what they believe about ghosts...

In my early OBE wanderings, I trekked around what I perceived to be my physical surroundings while in a non-physical state, and I saw many "ghosts" on the streets of San Francisco. Perhaps influenced by what Bob Monroe wrote about, I also saw that most of them just went about their business. One "guy" kept sweeping the front of a French restaurant. Another was walking his "dog." I saw no reason to bother them and they did not seem to notice me. I had not encountered the more "lively" variety up to this point...

When I saw these ghosts during my OBEs, they looked like slightly transparent living people, whereas when we surprised her on that mountain road in the middle of the night back in 1991, my friend and I were (once we realized what we were seeing) wide awake, and she looked very different. After comparing notes, my friend and I agreed that we both saw a classic Chinese ghost – long black listless hair (check), pale skin (check), dead pan expression (check), tattered white dress (check), no feet (check), and that stare... (check).

As I get ready to revisit Taiwan in the non-physical, I fully expected "ghost girl" to still look like what I saw more than 20 years before since ghosts are outside of time. I now understand that even though my friend and I both described seeing the same thing, it did not mean "she" was "real." I would now consider us seeing her as more of a "glitch in the matrix." Normally we would not have been able to see her, but it was Ghost Month and we were out there in the middle of the night so... we interacted and got a little entangled.

My decision to change from using OBE to "learn stuff" to "do stuff" was mainly motivated by the sympathy I have for the "hungry ghosts." Even as a child I always felt ghost stories set people up to be afraid with their scary music and "jump cuts." When considered in the context of narrative, most the ghosts are usually seeking justice or just want for the truth to come out about their deaths so then they can rest. Sure, the dead are hungry. Hungry for truth and justice! While I understand why people are afraid, to me, most ghosts are like that old children's cartoon, "Casper, the Friendly Ghost" - misunderstood... and only want to be friends. Well, be careful about that... Some ghosts make worse friends than drug addicts!

With ghosts, like OBE, fear will definitely make it bad even if it wasn't going to be.

In the case of Taiwan ghost girl... Well, we have already made our acquaintance in the physical world, and I have already given life (half-life maybe?) to a whole bunch of "ghost zombies" in the non-physical, so what have I got to be afraid of? Well, some people have a lot of fear because they believe you can get your astral body infected from working with "dirty things" by which they mean the "hungry dead." So they have entire sets of astral rituals once can learn for "cleansing" your astral body.

As an aside, let me take a minute to discuss the "astral body," as a subtle energy body as posited by many philosophers. Most place it somewhere in the intermediary between the immortal soul and the physical body, and see it as composed of a subtle yet still physical material. The concept ultimately derives from the philosophy of Plato where it is related to an astral plane. Traditionally "astral bodies" were viewed as traveling in and out of the "earthly plane," basically life on Earth, and into the "astral plane" which consists of the planetary heavens of astrology. The term was adopted by nineteenth-century Theosophists and neo-Rosicrucians.

The idea of astral body is often mixed up with ideas rooted in worldwide religious accounts of the soul's journey or "ascent" to heaven. Similar to the accounts from the modern day out-of-body experiences, the astral travelers leave their physical body and travel in their astral body into the astral realms, where there are all kinds of heavens, hells, and purgatorial existences. In this reckoning, it is often the expectation of the believers of each religious sect that give them their unique visions of heaven and hell. If upon death their expectations are met, this may simply be an astral projection of their beliefs into phenomena.

I disagree with conceptions of the astral body as an "aura" connected to the physical body that leaves the body during OBEs or astral projections. This supposed movement of the astral body around the real world is described in Muldoon and Carrington's book, "The Projection of the Astral Body." This concept traps believers in a form of neo-materialism which will simply not stand up to the science being done currently.

I prefer to imagine the process as an internal accessing of information. Instead of leaving a supposed attachment to the physical to travel in some "etheric" or "astral" plane, OBEs denote an internal experience of dream symbols, archetypes, memories, spiritual beings and visionary landscapes. As I became accustomed to the out-of-body state of consciousness, I found I needed to "travel" less and less and just "get" the information I am looking for.

I have started to formulate an idea that the "astral body" as internally perceived during an OBE is really our projection of the ego component of the personality. Any kind of OBE has the potential to be an ego-releasing or at least ego-lessening opportunity as it offers a chance to detach from one's physical body, the main source of ego identity. However, if the ego identity is simply shifted to what is perceived as the "astral body" the effect will become very limited. I suspect insufficient detachment to ego consciousness is a blockage to achieving the archetypal experiences readily available while out-of-body. The need to still see OBE as being focused on an astral body could arise from the desire to see it as another vehicle for ego consciousness. If this is true, the degree of attachment to one's ego consciousness will be reflected in how one's "astral body" is projected during an OBE.

Anecdotally, individuals with a strong sense of ego identity will tend to report astral bodies that look very similar to their own physical body. Tom Campbell and others have reported a state of being while out-of-body where there is no astral body, in fact, no body sensations at all. Vision is not "seen" through eyes, and sounds are not "heard" by ears. Tom calls it, "point consciousness." I have attempted many times to experience this and have clear descriptions of some of the signs to look for to let me know I have achieved it: 360-degree vision, pure awareness, no sense of a body, a powerful sense of unity with everything, but so far it is just a belief for me that such a state is possible...

In an archetypal dream I had soon after I began my Jungian training, I saw my physical body cut away and replaced with an energy body that a disembodied voice said was my "Bahá'í body." I found recalling this vision later informed my out-of-body travels in a powerful way. The image gave me confidence that I could do whatever I needed to because I have this "special" astral body. In hindsight I can see the link between how I processed this image into an ego-strengthening story and how this belief helped to derive the "abilities" I was intuitively able to manifest when I eventually undertook out-of-body travels.

As I developed confidence in these "astral" abilities, it further strengthened my ego identity with this astral image of "me". I continue to mostly experience my out-of-body state as having a body, by which I mean, the imagery, impressions, even emotions I have while in the non-physical are still processed and remembered as sensation that one receives with the five physical sensations. I see. I hear. I touch... even smell and taste, but clearly this is because of how I process the information, and not because that is how the information is actually coming to me.

My wife tells me the first time she experienced it, "point consciousness" was a big surprise to her; now it is something that she can access. For her, the experience is one where she has no body of any kind that she can tell. She is pure awareness. I have tried, but for now... Not my truth... yet.

I am beginning to see that one of the reasons this is not my truth yet is my very strong ego identification and occasional bout of ego inflation. Practically speaking, having that dream where I was granted a "Bahá'í" energy body probably planted a powerful subconscious suggestion that my "astral body" just got a big upgrade. Growing up, my image of astral body came from the Doctor Strange comic books. Stephen Strange, Mage Supreme, would "come out" of his physical body, which goes to sleep, and fight in his astral form. Well, my "Astral Body" seemed to have enough "life" to bring half-life back to a pack of zombies and all it did was make it sleepy. I felt I must be pretty powerful in my astral form

But in many ways this was another form of ego inflation, and as I describe later, it gets me in trouble as I pick on someone way too powerful for me. For now, I was focusing my intention on... Taiwan...

OBE: Putting an old acquaintance to rest

It was easy to focus on a place I know so well. Flying in, I recognize the single road leading up Yang Ming Mountain... I go into the ravine where she was supposed to have died when the bus she was riding in went over... Yeah, she's still here. This girl... such a sad story... the authorities were not able to find her body despite many attempts due to the rugged terrain, so she is still walking around... In my flying form, I zoom in and buzz around her like an insect... She starts to swat the air... So she can sense me... I stop and land, and become solid, and I guess to her perspective, I suddenly pop into existence.

Poor girl... exactly the same as I remember her... classic Chinese ghost, long black hair, pale face, white tattered dress... hey, this time, I can see her feet!

She panics and runs and tries to hide behind some bushes. I wonder if giving her bones some kind of marker would help... With that thought a white stone slab rises up from the ground... Seeing this, she panics some more and dives into the spot as if afraid I would do something to harm her remains. This is not working... I wonder if I can teach her to do the "Inner Sun?"

Okay, what I did next, I would not do now that I have more experience with this kind of thing. It was my first time… Later I found a video where Sadhguru specifically discusses why I probably shouldn't have been so… intrusive. But what I did was… I reach into the ground and pull up the skeletal remains… the bottom part remains stuck in the ground, and I only manage to pull out the skull and ribs. I sense the spirit shrinking into the skull, petrified… I pursue the spirit by reaching into her skull (it didn't occur to me at this point that no one likes having their head poked) mentally to transmit the Inner Sun technique. It takes but a moment and I tell the spirit hiding in the skull to try it…

Slowly, a tiny spark begins to shine inside the rib cage where the heart used to be and soon it becomes a bright light… the half skeleton is engulfed in the light… for a moment the light illumines everything then as it fades, I am left holding the moonlight and cool night air… I feel exhilarated. But, even then, there was a part of me that wondered if I didn't overdo it…

Setting aside any reservations, I was sure this was the right track. Helping spirits stuck after a traumatic death to move on can't be wrong, right? Wanting to really be up for the task, I spend two weeks preparing with more exercise and meditation than usual and less sugar and tea than usual. I also picked my next target with great care…

OBE: The murder house down the street

I remembered that five people were killed near my house in Ingleside, San Francisco, on the morning of Friday, March 23, 2012. The victims, all Chinese immigrants, were an elderly couple, two of their adult children, and their daughter-in-law. In Chinese-language media both in the United States and overseas, which devoted the most coverage to the killings, the case was usually referred to as the Lei family quintuple slayings.

Police initially believed the case to be a murder-suicide, but two days later arrested 35-year-old San Francisco resident Binh Thai Luc, a friend of one of the victims, and charged him with five counts of murder, five counts of robbery, and two counts of burglary. At his arraignment on April 5, 2012, Luc pleaded not guilty to the charges. Luc's trial finally began five years later on October 10, 2017. Following a seven-week trial and a week of deliberation, on December 11 the jury found Luc guilty of all the murder and burglary charges. Luc was subsequently sentenced to five consecutive life terms, one for each person he killed.

Close to home, don't have to fly too far… Jokes aside, it made sense. If any of the five people killed are still stuck there, they would want some help to "move into the light," right? There was good reason to think there might be "paranormal" activity. Soon after the murders the house was sold to a white guy who was interviewed by the Chinese media. He said he wasn't afraid and with the remodel, the place was a good deal. A few months later, he was interviewed again by the local Chinese TV channel when he put the house back on the market. He said it was because of, "you know, the noises… at night…" He would not elaborate.

The house, being in San Francisco, was bought instantly despite its history.

Without telling my wife what I was planning specifically, I told her I was going to sleep in the living room as the bedroom gets a little stuffy in the middle of the night now that we have to keep the door closed (we are cat-sitting and the stupid cat keeps wanting to go in the closet). She doesn't mind; easier for her to have OBEs alone in the big bed anyway…

I pop up with ease, entering the out-of-body almost before I intended to… Don't fly around the "real world" much, let's keep it slow, don't want to overshoot it… There's the house… What are these pillars of smoke doing outside? Are they keeping the spirits in the house from coming out? Should I "fight" them? No, wait… I don't understand this… I better go back…

The next night, I fly in again and the pillars of smoke are still there, but they sense me coming this time, and two of them seep into the cracks in the street to avoid me. I get it. The pillars are the spirits, and for some reason they are out in the street and not in the house… I intend to see them as they are… the two that went into the ground are drawn up and appear to me as an older Chinese couple… the two crouching by the garage appear to be young women… Let's get right to it, shall we? With my intention, I create a portal to "where they need to go…" It appears as a doorway of light to me… before I can even explain, the two women dart into it and they are gone…

The older couple don't want to go because... their son is still inside... I shift the portal to match the door frame of the house and show them that I am going to step through and go inside. I open the door and enter the house. The moment I am inside a man tries to hit me with a metal bat, fortunately the bat hits some kind of barrier before it strikes me and bounces off with such force the man is thrown backwards. I look at him and "remember" his story... gambling debts... his "friend," the debt collector was coming to talk to him... "Still no money? Your women can pay it off..." The last fight of his life... Beaten to death... Now they are all being beaten to death...

"So... the gambling man, eh?" I draw his attention to the open door, "Take a chance now. Just go through the door. It's got to be better than this... what are you waiting for?" I wave to the parents. "Your parents are on the other side waiting for you..." Seeing their son talking to me calmly instead of just wildly swinging his bat (no wonder they had to get out of the house), they rush forward and as they cross the door frame, they disappear. Their son then lets out a loud cry, and rushes past me towards the door. On impulse, I kick him in the butt and send him flying towards the door. The second before he goes past the portal, he turns and looks at me with a mixed expression of gratitude and embarrassment, and then he too disappears.

Silence... I stand for a full minute. Why am I still here?

This is odd. I focus my intention on seeing what is left to do in this house. I get a strong feeling there is something under the ground... something old.... Something that doesn't belong here...

I guess I will have to dig it out... I will need a tool... With that thought a long sword appears in my hand. With this tool, I stab into the floor and dig at the dirt underneath... After a bit of this, the earth starts to shake and a giant centipede-looking thing rises up from the rubble. It has two short antennae and its head is the size of a car. It bares two sharp fangs and towers over me. I start to stab at it with my sword and drive it back. It becomes fearful... It is harmless to me...

I put down the sword, and think I need to do something to help this thing pass on. Perhaps I can say a prayer or chant a spell or something? The first thing that comes to mind is a Cantonese Buddhist chant I learned as a child, "namo ami tuofo" (南無阿弥陀佛 Homage to Amitabha Buddha)," As I repeat the phrase, the "centipede" writhes in pain...

No, this is not what I want. Wait... maybe it's because I am not really Buddhist... I am a Bahá'í. I should recite the Greatest Name... I start chanting over and over, "Yá Bahá'u'l-Abhá" (O Thou the Glory of the Most Glorious!) The centipede calms down and starts to shrink in size, and soon its shape transforms as well. In a moment, it has become an alien-looking infant with two little antennae on its head. I gently pick it up and it looks up at me. I walk towards the door not sure what will happen, but as I pass through with the alien baby, it disappears It was a ghost too Not human would be my guess As I fly up to return to my body, I feel a sense of accomplishment and joy that I had never felt in all my non-physical travels up to that point.

The next morning, the weather was perfect. We went out and everywhere we got to, a parking space would be waiting. Feeling hungry, we dropped by my friend's shop. He has an amazing-looking sandwich on the counter. He tells me that he is introducing it to the menu and he just made this one to take a picture for advertising. He takes a picture then tells me to eat it. His treat. "Please eat it," he pleads...

And the treats kept coming all day long. It was like I was being rewarded in physical material reality for something I did in the non-physical.

A couple of months later, I am telling my sister while she is visiting us from Canada about my murder house adventures, and as just I get to the climax of the story, she and my wife both seem to lose interest and started looking out the window behind me. A little deflated at first, but then as they both exclaim, "Oh look!", I turn to see that it is suddenly drizzling around our house during an otherwise sunny day. There is a clear double rainbow that from where they are sitting would look like it was crowning my head. They tried to get a picture, they said, but it was something you had to see in the moment... Synchronicity.

Spirit release therapy

After what certainly appeared to me as a successful "release" of some human spirits and one non-human spirit from being "stuck," I decided to seriously research the subject in modern psychological literature. William

Baldwin's *Spirit Releasement Therapy: A Technique Manual*, published in 1995, was probably the watershed event for this movement. Dr. Baldwin left a successful dentistry practice to pursue his passion in spiritual healing, and it led to his doctoral dissertation in psychology on the subject. While I am sure many licensed psychiatrists and psychologists have discovered, often by accident, that this type of therapy works better than what they learned in medical or graduate school, Dr. Baldwin was the first to openly discuss how drug therapy only masks symptoms, and talk therapy reaches only as deep as the patient's conscious mind can go. His work helped to make the use of spirit release a legitimate therapy.

The successors of Dr. Baldwin, who died in 2004, generally identifying cases where spirit release should be used early during consultations. Many psychologists who use spirit release prefer to call the spirits, "entities," probably in order to differentiate what they do as much as possible from church-based exorcists and deliverance ministers. However, no matter how much they might want to avoid the label "medium," in service to their patients, these alternative therapists are breaking from materialistic science by treating the spirits as having an actual albeit immaterial existence.

Over the years, the case studies that have been published indicate that spirits come in several varieties. Most are "earthbound," those that are so attached to the loved ones they've left behind, or too addicted to one of the Earth's many vices, such as alcohol or narcotics to leave when their lives ended. Others are simply confused, not even sure they've died. Then there are reports of "dark force entities" that seem to be intent on evildoing. These attach themselves to unsuspecting mortals to inflict maximum damage to self-esteem, family relations and every expression of love.

One of the most extraordinary claims made by spirit release therapists is that nearly all of us, at one time or another, have had entities attached to us. Dr. Baldwin wrote that he did not intend to discover attached spirits in therapy, they emerged, unsought, out of the sessions. While still very much in the "alternative" section, more and more healers from licensed psychiatrists to less credentialed hypnotherapists are describing a spiritual cause to their clients' problems, and the same effective method of dealing with it. One might suspect a conspiracy except for the fact that the movement is so widespread, with practitioners working in clinics in all over the globe.

Proponents of this movement see spirit release not as a throwback to medieval times when those "demonically" possessed were ostracized or even put to death, but as an advance. William Woolger, an internationally renowned transpersonal psychologist, sees it as "the next and essential stage in the development of psychology, a kind of return to the source."

Dr. Shakuntala Modi sees proactive uses of the spirit release principle and recommends a "protection prayer" for her patients, to be repeated every night. Dr. Modi is not even certain that spirits are real, perhaps they are fantastic inventions made up by her patients' subconscious minds, but nevertheless, they might also be exactly what they seem to be, and claim to be. I suspect the more religiously minded practitioners of spirit release therapy will tend to believe that the spirits are real, but all who use the technique strongly agree that treating spirits as if they were real is the key the therapy's effectiveness. After a startlingly quick recovery from their immediate complaint, many of the "cured" clients will decide to take on some form of spiritual discipline to assist in their permanent recovery.

Of course, controversy lingers over spirit release's non-material basis, and Dr. Modi was sued for not fully disclosing the "religious" nature of her treatment to patients, and for insurance fraud. Interestingly, the Virginia state court agreed that while the treatment is to be considered "experimental" and Dr. Modi needed additional written consent from her patient, it also deemed the procedure "legitimate" and ordered the insurance provider to pay the full claim.

In my personal experience, there does indeed appear to be spirits attached to many people, mostly in benign ways, and some even serving as a companion of sorts. It is almost as if the psychic world is much like the materials world with its invisible micro-organisms that help and hinder our health. As I read more from the "spirit attachment" literature, I see many cases where a spirit is confused or simply out of fear does not go to where it needs to go. According to these writings, many spirits remain on the earth plane because of a lack of awareness of their own death.

Confusion, distrust and disbelief concerning religion and spirituality all can play a part in preventing the spirit from moving "into the light."

This body of literature is mainly generated by psychologists and hypnotherapists who use hypnosis to treat patients they consider to be suffering from "spirit attachment." According to their research, a person subjected to this experience may report hearing voices yet have no other psychotic symptom or behavior. Spirit attachment may also be apparent by the sudden onset of drug or alcohol usage, unusual and inappropriate speech patterns and behavior patterns, or noticeable personality changes.

Hypnosis is used to open up a safe communication with any entities that do not belong with a person and a therapeutic discussion ensues, allowing any unwanted energy to be gently returned to the place where they belong. spirit release is a form of therapy, not a rite. Unlike exorcism, it comes from a position of compassion, not confrontation. It aims both to free the client and to assist the attached spirit to continue its evolutionary journey.

Spirit release therapy, in its broadest sense, is any form of healing which "calls forth" and identifies earth-bound spirits, negative thought forms, dark energies and, upon occasion, what is described as demonic energies that can attach themselves to places and human energy fields.

Extensive records have been compiled on individuals who, after all other explanations have been exhausted, are treated for spirit attachment, or in extreme cases, possession. Symptoms include sudden changes in physical appetites for food, sex, alcohol, and drugs. Personal attitudes and beliefs can suddenly change, as can personal tastes. The voice and even facial features and appearance can alter dramatically. The records indicate an earthbound spirit can retain the psychic energy pattern of its own thinking, and can transmit to its "carrier" victim mental abnormality or emotional disturbance, as well as any symptom of physical illness. This condition can be extremely confusing and frightening for a person, and for friends and family. Attachment to any given person may be completely unplanned, even accidental. An attachment in rare instances can be benevolent in nature. More often it is self-serving to fulfill a personal need of the spirit.

Without going into an in-depth discussion of hypnosis here, let me quickly deal with the idea that the therapist is "suggesting" the narrative of spirit attachment to the hypnotized patient and therefore the whole of spirit release is bogus. The best evidence is found in cases where the spirits speaking through the hypnotized patient give information that the therapist does not know. And particular cases where the personal history of the spirit later checks out as accurate are hard to show as anything but authentic. By its nature, spirit release deals with spirits attaching to humans who can report on it under hypnosis. More advanced techniques involved using mediums that go under hypnosis and answer on behalf on the patient. Sometimes this is done with the consent of the patient, but without the knowledge of the patient, to avoid giving the medium any information in advance.

Some skeptics are still not convinced there are such things as spirits and if there is anything to this, it is probably split personality at work.

I, of course, have my own opinion because I have direct experience of dealing with a spirit attachment case involving a negative spirit affecting material reality. It didn't start out that way. I didn't go looking for it, and in fact, I had no idea it might have been a spirit attachment situation...

A Bahá'í friend had asked for prayers for her infant son on social media. I not only prayed, I also went out-of-body to see if there was more healing I could do in that situation. But every time I went there, all I could see was darkness. It felt like I was being blocked Still I sent healing intent as best as I could, and with all the prayers of the Friends, the little baby boy got better.

Only he was in emergency the next month, and his mother was again pleading for prayers and Divine assistance. It went on and on like that for over a year after I became aware and my friend's social media postings made it clear that it had been this way long before. The poor kid was in trouble. During this time, I experienced some events that I had no idea might be related, but oh, they were. One night, before falling asleep I get the distinct impression of a giant "hair monster" crawling on the ceiling over our bed. I had learned by now not to overreact to non-physical experiences, and I did nothing. It soon went away. I told my wife about it. She said she had seen worse. I forgot about it because I had seen worse too.

The little boy kept getting sick, we all kept praying, and I would keep trying to "see" if there was something I could do. One night, I saw a "vision" of the boy grown up. I tried to bring that vision back to the little boy now, but there was something blocking me...

A few days later, as me and my wife walked outside to get to our car which had been parked outside due to some need to keep the garage clear, I hear her stumble behind me. Within 10 seconds, her ankle had swollen up to the size of a tennis ball. Within one minute she could not walk. My wife said it was like she got pushed over. "There was a freaky guest of wind, and I just went down." My intuition flickered in a way that I imagine what "Spider Sense" would be like... But there was nothing to connect the feeling to...

I still didn't think there could be any linkage to any of these events. Then one night, "she" made it clear to me...

I go out-of-body again looking to help heal the little boy in the non-physical, but this time, I hear a gentle female voice in the enveloping darkness. It politely says, "I should have him. She has a healthy boy, a good boy. This is a sick boy, a sad boy. He belongs to me."

"Who are you?"

"I am a princess." The voice says proudly.

"What is your name?"

"I am the same as his mother." The voice is firmer.

"No, you are not his mother. You need to leave him alone."

"YOU need to leave us alone. I can do more..." The voice becomes shrill and louder.

"Do more... Are you the one making him sick?"

"I can do more... to her." The voice fades away.

I back off too. So, this was here the whole time. I focus my intent to see what is there... Hair and more hair... Black, long hair... Lots of it... Is it nothing but hair? No, there is someone in the middle of all that hair... She's blocking me... I will leave... For now...

Now I was convinced this is a spirit attachment situation. I am already involved. There was no going back. The allusion to "doing more... to her" made me think the spirit was hinting that she was responsible for my wife's fall. I need to find out if there is a living history to this spirit...

I researched her cryptic remark, "I am the same as his mother." The clue lay in the fact that while she is white, my friend was raised in Japan, and has a Japanese first name. I search for a princess with that name... There is only one in (not so) modern history. She was in the line that should have inherited the throne, but her brother died, and so it went to Hirohito's line. She died decades ago...

The situation matched cases that I had read about in spirit release literature. Except now it was personal.

"She" messed with my wife. The ankle will heal, and the pain and suffering is water under the bridge. But her threat to "do more..." made it personal...

I am not proud of what happened next, but I guess I made the same mistake my "higher self" did when emotions take charge. But this time, it was "me"... and I got a little carried away...

I went looking for a fight and she gave me one. Girding my loins for a fight, I lie down. Quickly going into the non-physical, I approached her, I used my intention to conjure the best weapon I could think of to fight someone like her, and it was... giant flaming scissors!

Yeah, it was the right tool. Hair monster... You are so done!

It wasn't much of a fight. Cutting and burning.... Cutting and burning... Cutting and burning...

I felt bad as soon as the fight was over. With all the hair that had protected her now destroyed, I see the princess lying on the ground. She looked young, and unconscious. Was she pretending? I drop the scissors and bend down, and let myself be open to an attack... No, she's "dead."

I feel like I could almost cry, but I think it would be strange since I am just going to put her into the light? I open the "where she needs to go" portal and put her frail body through... at the last moment before I let her go – she opens one eye and looks defiantly at me... And she's gone...

Previously I had only connected with what felt like spirits haunting a place. This time I felt "it" was in a longstanding connection to a living person, and the release was more than a release, it was more like... an exorcism. There was no good feeling when it was over... I was just tired and a little sad...

I tell myself there was no talking to her and the life of the little boy might have even been at stake, plus... I made it personal. Part of me recognized that I wanted to see what I could do in a non-physical fight. I beat her easily and I found it was no fun beating someone weaker than you. I know I could fight pretty well in the non-physical, and part of me was itching for a tougher fight. What were my limits?

My ego wanted to know...

I try to check in on the princess and after a long flight through a completely gray void, I arrive in a dark room and am surprised to see she has not been reborn. There was a soft light shining on her and she was sitting on a throne, her body sat still but her face was violently shaking back and forth, each shake revealing a different person, a different lifetime... It seemed as if it would take a long time for the lives to integrate... I will just go now...

Well, to close out the section on spirit release, I will recount the tale of how I went looking for trouble to test my "fighting limit" in the non-physical. I thought about challenging the toughest things I have encountered... the black-oil guardsmen? No, they work for "her" and I think I will just leave that head poker alone... Maybe I will challenge the 10-foot tall kaleidoscope-face guys? No, they are allies of humanity in their timeline it looked like... The big scary things are usually harmless unless you bring in your own fear... No point "fighting" your own fear...

Like my first Spirit Release attempt with the girl on Yang Ming Mountain, I went back to "reality" for source material. In the first book, I described a "bad dream" that I had in what I later learned was a haunted hotel. In the dream, I thought I woke and saw a solid shadow come out of a corner and try to possess my body. Now, that thing was a real nightmare. "It" seemed to really come into the room before I could realize it was a dream... It went back into the corner when I almost woke up. I used to think I "scared it off," but on deeper reflection, there was no sign of fear whatsoever in the thing when it left. "It" should be pretty strong...

I am also pretty sure there is a portal in that hotel to wherever it went...

Destination unknown...

I think I will go fight that thing...

At the time, it seemed like a great idea...

Not knowing what was in store, I went into the non-physical and went to the hotel... The portal is easy to see in the non-physical, you can't miss it... This one is dark for a change. Well, if dead people go through the light and get released, where will a living person like me go if I pass through a dark portal?

I don't even think about it... One giant leap later...

I come out in front of what looks like an ancient Chinese mansion with high walls and large trees growing all around. I see I had dressed myself in an "ancient warrior" outfit... I walk to the front of the mansion. It has a Chinese style moon gate. It is way too large for a human... And these tend to be reserved for the inner courtyard? Is this not the front door? The round opening is much larger than even a normal city gate and the red wooden doors in the middle are studded with golden bolts... there are faces carved onto the round heads... (are those expressions looking at me?)

I rush forward and kick the gates open looking for a fight.

As I charge in I see... an abandoned courtyard. Then my eyes are locked in on the far distance. Straight down along a tree lined path, I see the "thing," and now it had a human form. I knew instantly it was "him." He has his back to me and from this distance I could only see a black silhouette. Turning towards me, he waves his right hand, and five shadowy figures emerge from his hand, one from each finger, and begin flying my way. As they rush towards me, I see they appear to be made of black smoke, but are solid enough to each be holding weapons. I quickly materialize weapons of my own, giant flaming scissors and my trusty sword. The smoke "demons" seem to lose solidity if they move too fast so I leap into the air and taking advantage of my greater speed, press the fight to them. But to my chagrin, I found my weapons would just pass through their bodies when I scored a hit. While our weapons clashed in mid-air, I couldn't connect with the ones holding the weapons... I am barely holding my own against the five of them! We fight for several minutes...

I miss a beat and one of them kicks me in the chest... the blow passed right through, but it feels like I got the wind knocked out of me! This is new, but not in a good way. I have never felt anything like physical pain while out-of-body thus far... Then I remember that Bob Monroe wrote he once wrestled a shadow being in his own room for what seemed like hours and felt a lot of pain while they fought out-of-body (he was fine in the physical)...

Oh crap, what a terrible time to remember that!

In the far distance I detect the man-shaped shadow... smiling. His hand contracts and the five smoke-demons all attack at once!

I realized I had found my limit. With a focused effort I managed to drive them away and got back out the ridiculously large moon gate. They do not pursue me and the gate slams shut with a rush of wind. With a sign of relief, I pause to wonder who did I just pick a fight with? Even with the gate closed, I can still feel the power of the source of the five demons... Then words come into my mind, not sounds of the words, not image of the words, but just the meaning of the words... "The One who judges the dead..."

That power is far greater than what I can muster... for now...

I learned something... If you go looking for a fight, you will find it. Shaken up and stirred around after being bested by "hand puppets," I fly back through the dark portal and head home.

As I come back to my body, I feel thirsty. I get up and look for my thermos, but instead of the small table that is next to my bed, I see the root of what looks like a giant tree. I see that my entire side of the room has become a part of this tree. I laugh and turn to my wife, "honey, did you put this here?"

She has her back to me lying on her side... No answer... I am still... out-of-body? This is "Inception"...

Of course I am not back in my physical body! There can't be a giant tree here! Focus... back to the physical body... Now!

..."We could have been friends..." I hear the words come out of my mouth just as I am waking up in the body. But the voice is not mine. It sounds squeaky.

"What did you say?" My wife says, half awake, in the dimness of our physical material reality bedroom.

"I... didn't say anything."

Anyone who is familiar with Jung's conception of the "shadow," might recognize what I confronted could be interpreted as a manifestation my internal shadow archetype. However, when I sensed that it was much more powerful than my "self," it felt more like a representation of the collective shadow. In any case, I am going to wage peace with this particular representation of the shadow... That's diplomacy by another name.

For anyone thinking, "This guy is smoking something strong and writing fiction", sorry to disappoint, but smoking something strong actually shuts down OBEs, and does not create nor enhance them. So does sugar. So does alcohol. Eating meat is not going to help either. Coffee is a definite no (at least for some). As one of my wife's non-physical guides pointed out, "you have to clean your antennae." If there are people who can eat a lot of junk food and still have OBEs, I would be astonished at what they can do if they "cleaned their antennae."

My wife took the advice to heart. She went from two cups of coffee a day to half a cup. Thanks to her lead, I am also heading towards a full vegetarian diet.

After my "battle" with the princess, I resolved to not use force in future Spirit Release situations. I didn't get a good feeling afterwards, and I get the feeling she "resents" me now... With news of the little boy getting stronger, I was done with spirit release work for now.

OBE: Pet heaven.

However, it seems the spirits were not done with me. One night, as soon as I had closed my eyes and with no intention even of having an OBE, I see what looks like someone shooting a laser pointer at my closed eye lids. Something wants my attention? Sure, I'll go check it out...

By following the beam of light, I quickly go out-of-body. Turns out the source is very close, I barely lift out and find myself landing again in what looks like some backyard near my house. Don't recognize the area, but it sure is overgrown... There is a small shadow in the deep bushes... It hisses at me as I get closer... Oh, it's a dead cat.

It crosses my mind that the Bahá'í Faith teaches the human soul and the souls of animals are not of the same quality. It's so scared it probably won't go through a portal even if I make one. In fact, it already looks ready to run away

So how am I to interact with an animal spirit?

I draw closer and the shadow shrinks in fear and prepares to flee. I reach out with an intention to understand what I can do...

Suddenly I am flooded with emotions – FEAR LONELINESS HUNGER LOST RESIGNATION...

I am awakened by the feeling of tears streaming down my face. I raise my hands to wipe them away and I knew I had to do something.

The next day I decided to do some research on animal spirits The Bahá'í teachings say that no animal has the divine spark that makes humans seek the transcendent in life. Animals certainly have emotions (I got a taste), can feel pain and happiness, can even understand human communication sometimes, but that doesn't mean they have souls – that quality which only human beings have, the capacity for the intelligence, the insight and the spirituality necessary to forge a relationship with the Creator, transcend the physical world and achieve an eternal existence after death. The Bahá'í teachings point out that our souls set us apart from the natural world:

"The true man – is soul, not body; though physically man belongs to the animal kingdom, yet his soul lifts him above the rest of creation. Behold how the light of the sun illuminates the world of matter: even so doth the Divine Light shed its rays in the kingdom of the soul. The soul it is which makes the human creature a celestial entity!

By the power of the Holy Spirit, working through his soul, man is able to perceive the Divine reality of things. All great works of art and science are witnesses to this power of the Spirit. The same Spirit gives Eternal Life." – Abdu'l-Baha, *Paris Talks*

As for the animal spirit, 'Abdu'l-Bahá says, "The animal spirit is the power of all the senses. The distinctive virtue or plus of the animal is sense perception; it sees, hears, smells, tastes and feels. In it, the power of love, of attraction, reveals itself in certain emotions and sensibilities which produce instinctive fellowship and association. The animals are imbued with kindness and affinity which manifests itself among those of the same species."

He tells us that both animals and human beings have physical sensations and emotions, and so enjoins upon us to show the utmost kindness towards animals:

"Briefly, it is not only their fellow human beings that the beloved of God must treat with mercy, and compassion, rather must they show forth the utmost loving-kindness to every living creature. For in all physical respects, and where the animal spirit is concerned, the selfsame feelings are shared by animal and man. Man hath not grasped this truth, however, and he believeth that physical sensations are confined to human beings, wherefore is he unjust to the animals, and cruel.

And yet in truth, what difference is there when it cometh to physical sensations? The feelings are one and the same, whether ye inflict pain on man or on beast. There is no difference here whatever. And indeed ye do worse to harm an animal, for man hath a language, he can lodge a complaint, he can cry out and moan; if injured he can have recourse to the authorities and these will protect him from his aggressor. But the hapless beast is mute, able neither to express its hurt nor take its case to the authorities. If a man inflicts a thousand ills upon a beast, it can neither ward him off with speech nor hale him into court. Therefore is it essential that ye show forth the utmost consideration to the animal, and that ye be even kinder to him than to your fellow man.

Train your children from their earliest days to be infinitely tender and loving to animals. If an animal be sick, let the children try to heal it, if it be hungry, let them feed it, if thirsty, let them quench its thirst, if weary, let them see that it rests."

Selections from the Writings of 'Abdu'l-Bahá (p. 159.)

My Bahá'í friend tells me about a story of 'Abdu'l-Bahá once being asked a question about the departed spirits of beloved pets. Basically, what the questioner wanted to know was, do dogs go to heaven?

'Abdu'l-Bahá answered by saying that it depends on the life the owners of the dog gave to it while it lived because the heaven of the animal is created from the love of the human.

This gave me an idea. I will go back to the dead cat and create a portal not from the intention of "where it needs to go" like I usually would since that would probably just scare it away. Instead I will create a portal from my own love of animals. From the point of view of the little cat spirit, it should look like "heaven," or at least that is the idea...

I return to the spot... the shadow is still there, but looking weak... probably will dissolve back into elemental forms before long if I don't do something... I focus... A portal appears, and it does look different than the usual brightly lit rectangular doorway that comes out... its more pinkish and smaller... And oval-shaped...

The little shadow trots out from the bushes... it stops to check out the portal then heads right into it and disappears... soon other shadows come... mostly cats... a few small dogs...

After there are no more shadows, I go back and have a good sleep.

OBE: Letting go is the hardest part

I can't stay away from Spirit Release very long. I find a lot of meaning when I perceive I am helping a spirit move on. Even if the entire experience represents an internal psychological release of some trapped complex, it feels good, and as a practical matter, I am becoming more compassionate and more capable of overcoming egocentric thoughts and behaviors. I am on the right track.

I remember the family in New York's Chinatown that I wrote about in the first book. A mother and her four kids butchered by the father's cousin that they invited into their home. I cited the case as an example of what can happen when a simple mind frustrated with material failure and dead to the life of the spirit, tries to remove "the cause" of his emotional pain. His chilling confession that he killed them because he was jealous of his cousin did not qualify for an insanity defense, but is he really sane?

I go and look in at the situation... they are still there... the husband seems to want them to be there, and they don't want to go anywhere either... I leave them alone...

I try a few other people, due to the circumstances of their death, whom I suspect might not have passed on right away... I ran into more and more cases where the spirit recognized it was dead, but would not passed until some condition had been met...

Sadhguru talks about Spirit Release in some of his videos. He does so in his own cultural terms, but it is clear to me he is referring to the same psychological phenomenon. He advises that we should never intervene in the "evolution" of the spirit even if it is hanging on to someone since sometimes they are both hanging on to each other. He adds cryptically in one video, "but when it creates problems with the living, we go in and deal with it." I take that advice to heart and stop looking for spirits to release. But if it creates problems for the living...

One day, my friend who knows about my adventures in the non-physical realm asked me to look in on her granddaughter. She confesses that she is worried the little girl has some kind of "spiritual sickness." She makes little weird noises all the time... Plays with her "invisible friend" a little too much... When her parents took her for a check-up to see if there might be any underlying medical conditions, she completely freaked out when the doctor wanted to draw blood for tests... After three attempts, the parents had to give up on the blood tests. Apparently three adults could not restrain her sufficiently (without excessive force) on these separate occasions. The medical office told them not to come back until she is "psychologically ready."

I can see my friend is truly distraught and this seems to qualify as causing problems for the living. So, I do my thing...

I make my attempt while meditating one afternoon, and I barely have time to drop my body sensations when an image comes into focus. I see a little monkey-looking thing hanging on the little girl's back... like the expression, but literally. I look more closely... it's not a monkey... more like an underdeveloped human... it sees me...

"What is your name?"

"Bebe," it chirps, "Bebe."

"Why don't you come over here? It's a lot more fun than over there."

It jumps onto me... There is an electric shock feeling (not unpleasant) as the little humanoid merges into me and I am shocked back into the physical... I would have to categorize the sensation as a flash of bliss... That was new...

The whole experience is over in what feels like five seconds. I decide not to tell my friend that I saw anything, in fact, I decide the best thing was to tell her that I saw nothing since she already had this fearful image of "spiritual illness" in her mind. Intuition told me telling her the truth would only worry her more at this point, and the "problem" had already been "released."

However, as I am telling my friend the "little white lie," I perceive that the little underdeveloped human was a sibling to the little girl that it was hanging on to. An abortion… or a miscarriage…

A few days later, my friend reports that her granddaughter had "miraculously" relented and they were able to have her blood taken voluntarily. They found nothing wrong in her tests (of course), so they know it wasn't drugs in her system or some crazy medical condition.

At this point, I felt able to tell her the whole story including how the little spirit seemed to be a miscarried fetus. My friend was a little taken aback and said no, her daughter never mentioned anything like that, so it can't be. I say everything I see is metaphorical and to take it that way. Symbolic language and all that…

A couple weeks later, my friend tells me with some excitement that she asked her daughter if she had conceived other children that didn't come to term… (Wow, how do you work that into a conversation?) And her daughter confessed that she had… It was an accident with taking some meds that had a blood-thinning side effect… The baby was still so young… They hadn't given it a name yet… Her daughter said it was their first child and she used to rub her belly and just chuckle, "I have a bebe… he he… I have a bebe…" Then they lost the baby…

She never told her mother because it would have just made her sad… there was no reason to do that… so she never did… until she asked her about it…

I am a great admirer of William James. James (January 11, 1842 – August 26, 1910) was an American philosopher and psychologist, and the first educator to offer a psychology course in the United States. James was one of the leading thinkers of the late nineteenth century and is believed by many to be one of the most influential philosophers the United States has ever produced, while others have labeled him the "Father of American psychology."

Along with Charles Sanders Peirce and John Dewey, James is considered to be one of the major figures associated with the philosophical school known as pragmatism, and is also cited as one of the founders of functional psychology. Even more than a Jungian when it comes to psychological philosophy, I consider myself a "Jamesian."

As a pragmatic psychologist, what I am seeing is that there is a concurrence of my experience of a successful "release" of a disturbing spirit, and the person that was affected being relieved of their ailments. The person affected need not know the release is being attempted. Concurrence does not equal cause... However, if the concurrence is sustained and can be used as a treatment then by all means, use it.

Perhaps due to the uncanny timing of her granddaughter's improvement, my friend soon asked me to help someone else she knew. This person is a writer of high intelligence and had the means to take a long sabbatical to "think things through." She was traveling through town, and I later learned she had been in a severe state of depression for over a year following two miscarriages over a span of three years that culminated in the end of her marriage. We had lunch together and shared some polite small talk. Afterwards, my friend told me the details of her story and suggested I pray for her, and perhaps, "do the OBE thing..."

I prayed sincerely that this dear lady could recover from life's successive shocks and find her way back on her feet... Then I went out-of-body to see what I could see...

Since I already knew about the two miscarriages, I half expected to see something similar to the underdeveloped human, monkey-like shape I saw before. But when I went to look for her that night... locating the person by intention... I was surprised by the image that confronted me.

It looked like two tear-shaped globs of caramel were hanging off her back. One was the size of a loaf of bread and the other a small backpack. I reached out to see what their intentions were... They are feeding on her... They are feeding on her grief... No, she is feeding them... She feels she needs to grieve for them... She feels grieving for them is what a mother does... They would rather go and are ready to go... Not much else left to consider. It is not helping their mother to keep "feeding" them like this. They are just becoming big gum drops.

Well, if they are ready to go that makes it easy for me... With practiced intention, I open a portal right under them and I can sense it is will relief that they release their grip and drop right into the bright little rectangle...

A few days later, my friend tells me her writer friend is no longer depressed. Just before she left San Francisco, she reported that it was as if "a weight had been dropped from her shoulders."

The mechanism for the alleviation of symptoms obtained from Spirit Release Therapy is disputed, but my OBEs validate what the wealth of Spiritual Release literature obtained by hypnosis describes. In some of the cases, the patient is not even aware that they are the subject of a medium under hypnosis doing spirit release on them in a remote location. Pretty much what I am doing except I am not in a hypnotic state... No, I totally am not! OBEs are on a difference level of consciousness... If you don't believe me, try experiencing it yourself...

Every traditional culture has mediums and methods for contacting and appeasing the departed. Is it just a feature of the human mind to have a need for such contact, so someone will rise to fill the job, or is it rather, the need is a recognition of something reaching out from beyond the grave to give us a message?

When I was very young, my dad got really sick. Then he got well. It was only years later that I understood more about the events that transpired between him getting sick and recovering. What happened was that after seeing both Chinese and Western doctors and not getting any results, my parents consulted a "rice whisperer," who used, you guessed it, different colored rice, in his communications with the "great beyond."

He got a message right away. My dad has an older brother who died as a child. He is envious of my dad having a wife and family, and his being denied one, and so... he's "making" my dad sick. Remedy – ghost bride. Find a girl who died single and has a suitable horoscope then arrange with her family to do a "ghost wedding." They do that... My dad is still sick? Back to rice whisperer...

My "ghost uncle" is still pissed that he has no son to carry his family line, and so... my dad is still sick. Remedy – Make my eldest brother called our uncle his "dad."

No. He's not doing it. They make my number two brother do it. He is more compliant, but my dad is still sick! Back to rice guy one last time! Answer from the rice... "A second son won't take a second son." Dead and still so demanding...

My parents never told me all the details of how they got my ghost uncle to finally relent, but apparently they had to officially change the written record back in our ancestral village to reflect the "change of parental authority," and, of course, burn a bunch of "hell money" to appease the guy. Soon after all the rituals were performed, my dad got better. This is what you can call spirit release therapy Cantonese style!

I was just a little kid then... Now I could have saved them the money they spent on the rice whisperer. Sorry, uncle, time to go to "where you need to go," here is the portal, don't make me make you...

Please don't call me a "Ghost Buster." Totally different movie. "Ghost Releaser" sounds kinda kinky... "Ghost Whisperer" is taken... Maybe I will call myself the "Ghost Usher..." Wait, that sounds like Usher is dead. What is it I am trying to do? I imagine I am guiding spirits to their rightful places... Got it, Ghost Guidance Counselor.

And if counseling doesn't cut it, there's always the giant flaming scissors...

Chapter Five

YOU HAVE TO HAVE FAITH

Everything I have learned have led me to conclude that reality is as Baha'u'llah affirmed it to be:

God created humanity out of love. Humanity's purpose is to know and to love God in return. The aim of this life is to acquire faith, love of God, and other spiritual qualities in preparation for the eternal life to come. For in reality we are spiritual beings, and this material existence is only a prelude to our future life.

Baha'u'llah stated that it is impossible for us to completely understand the nature of the life beyond. No matter how many OBEs one might have, one still cannot possibly imagine something different from anything we have ever experienced while still connected to earthly existence.

Baha'u'llah makes this point in striking fashion when he writes, "The world beyond is as different from this world as this world is different from that of the child while still in the womb of its mother." – *Gleanings from the Writings of Baha'u'llah*, p. 157.

This analogy is worth pondering. The purpose of life in the womb is to prepare the unborn child for life in the outer world. During this time the child develops senses and capacities that are necessary for its continued existence and prosperity. All the while the child is oblivious to this fact. Even if there were some way it might imagine a "life to come," how could the child ever truly comprehend the vastness and wonders of the world beyond its mother's womb?

The same is true of the world beyond this one. If we face death with fear and trepidation, it is only because we, like the unborn child, are ignorant of what awaits us. In *The Hidden Words*, Baha'u'llah says:

"I have made death a messenger of joy to thee. Wherefore dost thou grieve?"

Baha'u'llah taught that every human being possesses a rational soul, the true seat of our personality and consciousness. The soul survives physical death and exists forevermore in the world of the spirit. This concept is easy to grasp intellectually, but the soul can never be understood intellectually, especially since the soul cannot be perceived with our senses in the same way that we can observe and understand physical phenomena. It is extremely hard for some people to imagine how it could be possible to continue to exist after death. These difficulties cause many to doubt the existence of the soul and of the life hereafter.

Baha'u'llah offers reassurance and addresses the question directly:

"Thou hast asked Me whether man, as apart from the Prophets of God and His chosen ones, will retain, after his physical death, the self-same individuality, personality, consciousness, and understanding that characterize his life in this world. If this should be the case, how is it, thou hast observed, that whereas such slight injuries to his mental faculties as fainting and severe illness deprive him of his understanding and consciousness, his death, which must involve the decomposition of his body and the dissolution of its elements, is powerless to destroy that understanding and extinguish that consciousness? How can any one imagine that man's consciousness and personality will be maintained, when the very instruments necessary to their existence and function will have completely disintegrated?

Know thou that the soul of man is exalted above, and is independent of all infirmities of body or mind. That a sick person showeth signs of weakness is due to the hindrances that interpose themselves between his soul and his body, for the soul itself remaineth unaffected by any bodily ailments. Consider the light of the lamp. Though an external object may interfere with its radiance, the light itself continueth to shine with undiminished power. In like manner, every malady afflicting the body of man is an impediment that preventeth the soul from manifesting

its inherent might and power. When it leaveth the body, however, it will evince such ascendancy, and reveal such influence as no force on earth can equal. Every pure, every refined and sanctified soul will be endowed with tremendous power, and shall rejoice with exceeding gladness."
Gleanings from the Writings of Baha'u'llah, pp. 153-154.

Many other passages like this one describe the heavenly joys to come. But they also make clear that happiness in the spiritual world is dependent upon certain conditions. It comes when we live up to what God expects of us in this world. We must, as Baha'u'llah puts it, walk "in the ways of God."

These ways are not the moral codes of the social status system you happen to be born into. They come from deep within you. It is about recognizing the truth when you see it because you recognize it within yourself. Truths such as, "That which you hate to be done to you, do not do to another."

In the non-physical world everything seems to run on intention. You can't hide your intentions or even censor them, you think it and it happens. In this world, I would have to agree with Margaret Mead when she said, "Never doubt that a small group of thoughtful, committed citizens can change the world; indeed, it's the only thing that ever has."

This world runs on faith. However, if that faith is placed upon the shifting sands of public approval or some unyielding doctrine blindly handed down generation upon generation, it will not serve you well. Or even worse, when faith is subverted to political ends and the faithful are manipulated into acting out of hate and ignorance, then all you have is blind faith in the "magical thinking" that what you believe makes it true.

Despite all materialistic evidence to the contrary, you have to have faith in your own immortality. You walk an eternal path.

Many people profess faith. They say I believe! They say I know I am an immortal spirit. But if you truly are an immortal spirit, would you despoil nature for financial gain? If you are an immortal spirit could you watch your fellows beings suffer and die while you just idle away? If you could touch your immortality, even if just for a moment, could you live just for yourself?

There is a poem by Ruhiyyih Khanum titled, "This is Faith." It begins with these lines:

To walk where there is no path,
To breathe where there is no air,
To see where there is no light-
This is Faith.

Indeed, if we are not just our bodies, we can truly walk where there is no path, breathe where there is no air, see where there is no light, and much more. Have faith that if you "clean your antennae," meditate, experience that you are not your body, or your emotions, or your thoughts, and that everything is energy and so are you, then you too can make the one giant leap into a consciousness that will touch upon a part of you that feels... immortal. You can see that you walk an eternal path. You can see that you don't need all that material stuff.

Speaking of faith and material stuff Let me tell you how a kid who grew up in ultra-materialistic Hong Kong with Taoism at home and Christianity at school ended up becoming a Bahá'í

Why be Bahá'í?

After coming to America at the age of 11, I learned to store all "cultural-religious" stories in the same place in my mind – interesting references having little to do with everyday life reality. Monkey King. Moses. Jesus and the miracle of all that bread (and fishes)! Jehovah has witnesses?

My first inkling that there was more meaning to these stories than as source material for science fiction was seeing Joseph Campbell on television presenting his book, *The Hero with a Thousand Faces*, (first published in 1949.) "Faces" is a work of comparative mythology by the late American mythologist. In this television presentation, Campbell discussed his theory of the journey of the archetypal hero found in world mythologies in such a captivating manner that it affected me deeply. Many others have confessed to being similarly affected by Campbell's theory and it has been consciously applied by a wide variety of modern writers and artists. The best known is perhaps George Lucas, who has publicly acknowledged Campbell's influence on the Star Wars films.

It was around the same time as the "Faces" program was airing that I saw a captioned photo about the Bahá'í temple in India being completed ahead of schedule

The "Lotus Temple," located in Delhi, India, is a Bahá'í House of Worship that was dedicated in December 1986, costing about $10 million. Notable for its flowerlike shape, it has since become a prominent attraction in the city. Like all Bahá'í Houses of Worship, the Lotus Temple is open to all, regardless of religion or any other qualification. The building is composed of 27 free-standing marble-clad "petals" arranged in clusters of three to form nine sides, with nine doors opening onto a central hall with a height of slightly over 40 meters and a capacity of 2,500 people. The Lotus Temple has won numerous architectural awards and has been featured in many newspaper and magazine articles. In 2001 it made the list of top ten most visited buildings in the world.

I was quite impressed with the photo. And ahead of schedule... in India... doesn't match what I am learning in my International Relations classes about what that country is like...

I ask my number two brother because he reads up on weird stuff. Hey, what's this Bahá'í Faith? He tells me it is a "middle-eastern mystery religion." I file that away in that place where I put Joseph Campbell

My dad died in 1993, I don't think about God. UFOs come and go, I don't think about God. Fall in love, fall out of love, I don't think about God. Then while serving at the American Embassy in Beijing, I overhear a snippet of a conversation "Did you know the head of finance is a Bahá'í?"

It was like a little bell went off in my head. That word had a power that I never recognized before. I seek out the head of finance for a friendly grilling on his religion. He welcomed it as any good Bahá'í would. We were both intellectually inclined so for a few months our conversation covered the full range of theocratic theory and he presented his understanding of the teachings.

After I ran out of questions, I asked to meet the community to see for myself if they practiced what they preached. The Bahá'í community in Beijing in the late 1990s was an interesting mix of people. Every 19 days, there would be a gathering; a "feast," they called it. It was usually at the home of a wealthy Persian businessman who had settled in China a few years earlier and was running a successful business. His residence was large enough to host the nearly 100 or so people who would regularly attend these affairs. The first time I went to a feast at his home I was impressed by the diversity of people. Although the Bahá'í Faith is not recognized as an official religion in China, there were no restrictions on Chinese citizens attending these feasts and well over half the attendees looked to be local people. The rest were an eclectic group Egyptians Malaysians Americans Canadians I lost count of the countries represented. The attitude of shared community was very strong. The conversation was stimulating. Then I forgot everything else once dinner was served

If you have never had the pleasure of high-quality homemade Persian food, then you need to!!!

I considered myself pretty cosmopolitan in my culinary experiences up to this point. Even had Ethiopian once in college! But I knew next to nothing about Persian cuisine.

The unique Persian culinary style has absorbed historical influences from the cuisines of its neighboring regions, including that of the Caucasus Mountains, Turkish cuisine, Greek cuisine, Central Asian cuisine and even aspects of Russian cuisine. Typical Iranian main dishes are combinations of rice with meat (such as lamb, chicken, or fish), vegetables (such as onions and various herbs), and nuts. Fresh green herbs are frequently used, along with fruits such as plums, pomegranates, quince, prunes, apricots, and raisins.

Characteristic flavorings such as saffron, dried lime, cinnamon, turmeric, and parsley are mixed and used in some special dishes. In the case of my first time to try Persian cuisine, I found out later (told humorously) that the dishes were "extra special" because the ingredients for these dishes were prayed over the night before so that the people who ate them would be well-fed in body and their spirits would also be "nurtured with the love of God."

But I didn't know any of this back then...

All I knew then was... it was... literally... the best meal I have EVER had.

Where has THIS been all my life??

I kept going back. I told myself it was mostly for the food. But I wasn't fooling myself… it was for everything that the group represented to me. A community that practiced exactly what it preached. I realize in hindsight, it was a moment in time that was rather unique. The non-Chinese members were mostly "pioneers" who had come to China in order to specifically fulfill a "missionary"-like purpose (although they are completely self-funded) announced by their supreme institution. These people were "on fire," and on their best behavior.

China has occupied a large space in the collective imagination of the world Bahá'í community ever since the early 20th century. This often-cited quote from Abdu'l-Bahá reflects these sentiments:

"China, China, China, Chinaward the Cause of Baha'u'llah must march! Where is that holy sanctified Bahá'í to become the teacher of China! China has most great capability. The Chinese people are most simple hearted and truth seeking. The Bahá'í teacher of the Chinese people must first be imbued with their spirit; know their sacred literature; study their national customs and speak to them from their own standpoint, and their own terminologies. He must entertain no thought of his own, but ever think of their spiritual welfare. In China one can teach many souls and train and educate such divine personages each one of whom may become the bright candle of the world of humanity. Truly, I say they are free from deceit and hypocrisies and are prompted with ideal motives."

"Had I been feeling well, I would have taken a journey to China myself! China is the country of the future. I hope the right kind of teacher will be inspired to go to that vast empire to lay the foundation of the Kingdom of God, to promote the principles of divine civilization, to unfurl the banner of the Cause of Baha'u'llah, and to invite the people to the Banquet of the Lord!"

From diary of Mirza Ahmad Sohrab, (April 3, 1917) quoted in *Star of the West* Vol. 21

Now after almost a century of decline, foreign invasion, partition by warlords, two revolutions, internal chaos, and military confrontation with both superpowers, China was interested in the world again, and the Bahá'í have come to "invite the people to the Banquet of the Lord!"

My Bahá'í friends in Beijing were some of the happiest people I have ever known.

The Chinese members were a mix of highly interested seekers (who probably tell themselves the come for the food), and new Bahá'ís. It was a bit complicated administratively since in compliance with Chinese law, the Bahá'ís Faith has no official administrative body inside China to register anyone wishing to declare their membership. However, in compliance with spiritual law you can have faith in whatever you want. And I met many Chinese who said they had declared in their heart and to their new faith community and that was good enough for them. They did not need an ID card to tell them their identity.

Of course, I, being the seasoned diplomat and natural-born cynic, began to wonder which of the Chinese members of our little spiritually minded community in the capitol of the largest officially atheist country in the world might be... spying on the rest of us.

It was no secret. The Chinese government is concerned about foreign subversion and sends security personnel to infiltrate suspect gatherings. Religious groups are particularly suspect for historical and ideological reasons. And if the security services weren't that interested in the Beijing Bahá'ís, well, the American Embassy is now sending two guys to their meetings!

And that Chinese-American guy, what is he going to tell the Chinese citizens who go to these meetings? Inquiring minds need to know. What they mainly needed to know was would Chinese Bahá'ís be required to give their allegiance to a foreign power whether religious or political.

Who really "runs" the Bahá'ís anyway?

What I learned was that "The Universal House of Justice" is the supreme governing institution of the Bahá'í faith. It is a legislative institution with the authority to supplement and apply the laws of Bahá'u'lláh, the founder of the Bahá'í Faith, and exercises a judicial function as the highest appellate institution in the Bahá'í administration. The institution was defined in the writings of Bahá'u'lláh and 'Abdu'l-Bahá, Bahá'u'lláh's successor, and was officially established in 1963 as the culmination of the Ten Year Crusade, an international Bahá'í teaching plan. The Seat of the Universal House of Justice and its members reside in Haifa, Israel, on the slope of Mount Carmel.

As for who might have been a spy? Well, I could not tell. I could not even come up with a top suspects list. They all seemed so sincere. After being in what I loosely defined as my "spiritual community" in Beijing for few months, I developed a strong emotional bond with a core group of Bahá'í friends. Still I wasn't going to "declare" anything like I was joining a religion. Then my friends suggested I pray. Prayer was not something I did a lot of back then.

From my experience in Hong Kong as a child, it was something the teachers made you say. In the army, it was something you do to get you through hardship. In the face of death, it is what won't come true.

Now I am supposed to pray for knowing the truth? Sure, I will read some prayers every night before bed and then think about it. That qualifies, right? So I do that, on and off, for a couple months.

Then I have a "religious experience."

I do not hear a voice. I do not see a vision. There is no physical sensation to speak of. But something within me changed as a result of those months of contemplation and asking for answers. There was a sense of confirmation. THIS is what I believe.

After that I declared to my friends, and a little later, I "came out" to the whole community. I had become another Bahá'í who didn't need an ID card to have his faith confirmed. For a time, I was happier than I'd ever been. I too was "on fire." I was soon able to officially register when the State Department transferred me to Hong Kong where the Faith was introduced during the lifetime of Bahá'u'lláh.

Hong Kong's history as a crown colony of the United Kingdom and then a special administrative region of the People's Republic of China has given it a unique history. As a commercial center and relatively open city even in the 1870s, Hong Kong became a location where non-Chinese Bahá'ís could settle and earn a living in trade or other commercial activities. The first Bahá'í in China was a Persian trader, who was recorded as having lived in Shanghai in 1862, and in 1870, this person was joined by his brother and they established a trading company.

Hong Kong was a frequent transit hub throughout the early 1900s for western Bahá'ís traveling to China and other parts of Asia. Among these travelers was Martha Root who started traveling in 1924. On several subsequent trips, she met with editors, librarians, and the president of Hong Kong University. She was interviewed on radio, spoke at Hong Kong University and had wide press coverage with several articles written about her visit in local papers.

Association with so many Bahá'ís from other lands gave heart to the Hong Kong Bahá'í expatriate community and demonstrated to the first Hong Kong Bahá'ís the reality of the global community that they had became a part of. Charles Duncan, Knight of Bahá'u'lláh to Brunei, recorded of this period that a number pioneers moved to Hong Kong and that slowly a community was built up consisting of resident pioneers of Indian, British and Southeast Asian backgrounds. He indicated during this time there was also a constant stream of Bahá'í visitors from abroad. Only two Chinese Bahá'ís, Pei Tswi, who lived in Hong Kong for a decade from the late 1920s, and Liu Chan Song, known to have resided in Hong Kong just prior to the Second World War, are recorded for this period.

Starting in 1953 there was a concerted effort to establish a permanent community of Bahá'ís in Hong Kong and with dedicated efforts this was accomplished by the mid-1950s. The enrollment of four new members allowed the Hong Kong Bahá'ís to form their first Bahá'í Local Spiritual Assembly (LSA) in 1956. At the beginning of 1957 there were only 14 members in the Hong Kong Bahá'í community. The LSA was registered with the Hong Kong government as a recognized "society" on 29 May 1958, and officially incorporated in 1969. These registrations were transferred to the National Spiritual Assembly when it was formed in 1974.

By 1961 there were approximately 60 Bahá'ís in Hong Kong and three Local Spiritual Assemblies. Much of the growth was assisted by pioneers of Chinese background from the Malaysian Bahá'í community who with their ability to speak the local language could best help in making contacts with the Chinese community living in Hong Kong.

When I was four years old, the Hong Kong Bahá'ís established a center which officially opened in August 1968. And when I left Hong

Kong for the United States in 1974 there were five local assemblies in Hong Kong. 1974 proved to be a pivotal point in the history of the Hong Kong Bahá'ís as the Universal House of Justice decided it was time for the Hong Kong Bahá'ís to establish a National Spiritual Assembly. The formation of a National Assembly in Hong Kong was the culmination of dreams and efforts commenced some 104 years before and it was a cause for great celebration in the Bahá'í communities of Hong Kong and elsewhere.

In the years since the formation of the national assembly, the Hong Kong Bahá'í community continued to expand. By 1979 it had grown to 10 local assemblies and a total of 26 localities. By 1991 there were 22 local assemblies in Hong Kong.

Despite the agreement to transfer sovereignty of Hong Kong to the People's Republic of China in 1997 and its designation as a special administrative region, the position of the Bahá'í administration in Hong Kong – its administration, membership and communities – in the context of local laws has remained unchanged. The "National" Spiritual Assembly is now referred to as the "Spiritual Assembly" or "Main Spiritual Assembly" in Chinese and still retains jurisdiction over the Local Spiritual Assemblies in Hong Kong. It is elected from the generality of Bahá'í residents in the community of Hong Kong.

Like numerous communities around the world, the Hong Kong Bahá'í Community undertakes community-building activities. These mainly consist of devotional meetings for adults, children's classes, junior youth groups, and circles of study, open to all, that enable people of varied backgrounds to meet and explore the application of spiritual teachings to their individual lives.

The Hong Kong Bahá'í Community, together with the Macau Bahá'í Community, frequently act as liaison and contact points with the Government of the People's Republic of China since there is still no administrative structure for the Bahá'í Faith operating in mainland China. It also leads events and activities that promote religious and societal unity and advancement. I was privileged to serve on a Local Spiritual Assembly and later on the National Spiritual Assembly while stationed in Hong Kong. I was especially happy to have been involved in reviving Bahá'í organization of the annual commemoration of World Religion Day which calls attention to the harmony of the various religions' spiritual principles and to emphasize that religion is a main motivating force for world unity.

When I left the city in 2001, the Bahá'í population of Hong Kong, while organically ebbing and flowing, had grown to about 3000. It was a time for me of stepping into greater social maturity, confirming I could offer some service in the promotion of principles I hold dear to my heart. However, given the peripatetic nature of my employment at the time, it was only a matter of time before I had to part ways with the Friends in Hong Kong.

Since I was very active in organizing events for the Bahá'í community to interact with non-Bahá'ís, I met a lot of people who came to Bahá'í events to socialize more than out of interest in the faith. There were attractive members of the opposite sex interested in me, and I was looking to get married, but it was complicated

After two failed engagements, one where I was the "bad guy" and another where I was the "sucker," I was in all honesty, gun-shy when it came to lifetime commitments. Just dating for "fun" the way I used to was not part of my plan. The Bahá'í teachings to not indulge in sexual relations outside of marriage was part of what I signed up for so, it had been awhile

When I became a Bahá'í in Beijing and stopped drinking alcohol, I lost a few friends who thought I had become too "religious." When I admitted that I was not going to have sex outside of marriage anymore, they thought I had joined a cult. The woman I was seeing while I learned about the Faith, "friend-zoned" me, but later, after returning to the US, she became a Bahá'í.

The teaching is very clear...

"Enter ye into wedlock, that after you someone may fill your place. We have forbidden you perfidious acts, and not that which will demonstrate fidelity." - Baha'u'llah (cited in *Promised Day Is Come*, par. 256)

There were one or two possibilities in the Bahá'í community, but before anything could develop, I was transferred from Hong Kong back to mainland China, and left behind me the high social profile and frenetic lifestyle that I still fondly remember. Back in mainland China, with no administrative order, Bahá'í activities were more limited and compared to Hong Kong, the concentration and number of Bahá'ís was also fewer. While I missed the closeness of the Hong Kong community, I admit I was glad to have more time for other pursuits. Realistic about how much teaching opportunities are limited in the mainland, I decided to concentrate on developing deep friendships with a few friends who were interested.

Fewer activities and meetings meant I actually had time for night classes... Three years of Jungian training and many hours of analysis helped me understand that much of my piety in the past was a form of ego inflation. I am so good... compared to that guy... compared to how bad I could be... I could see that the ego's defense of its own privileged position as the center of attention was to take on the colors of the "spiritual person." Allied with more primitive aspects of personality that lurks on the border of "Id consciousness," egocentric behavior continues to win the day, sabotaging any movement towards real awakening. Drastic action was called for...

So, I decided to take the road less traveled. I started with quitting my job as a diplomat. Then I moved in with my mom. Massive ego deflation. Self-isolation and even mild depression follow.

At a low point psychologically, my chance for the Baha'i Pilgrimage arrived. It had been quite a few years since I first applied and the notice caught me by surprise. Good thing my mom was stabilized now and it would only be nine days plus travel. My mom was a little incredulous that I was actually going to pay to a lot of money to "fly half-way around the world to pray."

Yes, I had been waiting a long time to do just that...

Personal Interlude: Queen of Carmel

In November of 2006, I fly halfway around the world, breaking my old record set during my Foreign Service days of 21 hours in the air with a new personal record of a coma-inducing 26 hour flight (with transfer).

Still, I feel exhilarated upon arriving in Israel and have no trouble continuing by train onto Haifa. My destination is Mount Carmel.

Mount Carmel is considered a sacred place for Bahá'ís around the world, and is the location of the Bahá'í World Centre and the Shrine of the Báb. The Shrine of the Báb is the iconic structure where the remains of the Báb, the founder of Bábi Revelation and forerunner of Bahá'u'lláh in the Bahá'í faith, have been laid to rest. The Báb was a merchant from Shiraz in Qajar, Iran, who in 1844, at the age of 24, claimed to be a messenger of God. He took on the title of the "Báb," Arabic for "Gate" or "Door," in a reference associated with the promised "Twelver" Mahdi or al-Qá'im. He faced opposition from the Persian government, which eventually executed him and tens of thousands of his followers, who were known as Bábís.

The Báb composed numerous letters and books in which he stated his claims and defined his teachings. He introduced the idea of He whom God shall make manifest, a messianic figure who would bring a greater message than his own. While the ultimate settling of the Bahá'í holy places in Haifa might seem to have historical roots in Baha'u'llah's imprisonment by the Ottoman Empire which then ruled Palestine, the shrine of the Báb's precise location on Mount Carmel was preordained by Bahá'u'lláh.

In the mid-19th century, a Protestant sect from southern Germany, calling themselves the Templers, settled in Haifa under the leadership of their Pastor Christoph Hoffmann. The Templers believed that by living in the Holy Land, they would hasten the second coming of Christ. They had calculated that the coming would happen on Mount Carmel. The Templers built a colony in keeping with strict urban planning principles and introduced local industries that brought modernity to Palestine, which had long been neglected by the Ottomans. They were the first to organize regular transportation services between Haifa, Acre and Nazareth, which also allowed for mail delivery. The restored old German Colony's red-roofed buildings lining the main road between Mount Carmel and the Mediterranean Sea now stand as a symbol of the city and have become the center of Haifa nightlife.

The area where the Templers waited for the second coming was designated by Bahá'u'lláh himself as the resting place for the Báb's remains, and they were laid to rest on March 21, 1909, in a six-room mausoleum made of local stone. The construction of the shrine with a golden dome over the mausoleum was completed in 1953, and a series of decorative terraces around the shrine were added in 2001. Some experts believed the terraces were "impossible" to maintain due to the high gradient of the slope of Mount Carmel and predicted they would collapse in the first major rainstorms. Eighteen years and counting

The completion of the terraces and the lighting event featuring the golden dome of the Shrine of the Báb are remembered in a song entitled, "Queen of Carmel," written to honor the sacrifice of generations of believers who contributed to make real the dream of completing this great work. Bahá'u'lláh, writing in the Tablet of Carmel, designated the area around the shrine as the location for the future administrative headquarters of the Bahá'í Faith, and these administrative buildings were later duly constructed adjacent to the decorative terraces, and are referred to as the Arc, on account of their physical arrangement. The Shrine, the Arc, and associated building around Haifa are collectively referred to as the Bahá'í World Center.

While on Pilgrimage, I had many opportunities to pray and meditate in the shrine and to rest in the shaded areas of the terraces. One day I was enjoying a quiet moment by the fountain pool on the ninth level, and I notice a furry blur darting across the footpath. It is long. A good six feet from nose to tail What was that animal? Later I asked one of the local gardeners and he said it was a giant mongoose. The gardener said they love the mongoose because they scare away the snakes. They come into the terrace for the water and to get away from the city. I was amazed that at the gardens could shelter such large wildlife, and the gardener commented that he was not a Bahá'í, but working there was like being in a "paradise."

The most interesting part of the journey to Haifa for me was the many Bahá'í holy places in and around Acre. They originate from Bahá'u'lláh's imprisonment in the Citadel during Ottoman rule. We visited the sparse stone cell where Bahá'u'lláh spent his first years in Acre. Digital photos that I took in the cell later revealed several strange translucent orbs. It was the only place during the entire trip where that happened. The final years of Bahá'u'lláh's life were spent in relative freedom residing in the Mansion of Bahjí, just outside Acre. Even though he was still formally a prisoner of the Ottoman Empire, his status among his jailers had risen considerably. Bahá'u'lláh died on 29 May 1892, in Bahjí, and the Shrine of Bahá'u'lláh is the most holy place for Bahá'ís; the location we face when saying the daily prayers. There is a threshold where one can actually see the container for the remains of Bahá'u'lláh. I had thought long and hard about what I would pray for when I got there

When I finally actually kneel down at the threshold, I try to keep only one thought in my mind as I pray, "I will to will Thy Will…"

I must confess I did not have anything resembling a "religious experience" while on Pilgrimage and I was not expecting to. The whole thing was pretty heavily scheduled and I was jet-lagged through half of it… On some level, I might have even felt I was just fulfilling an obligation of my faith…

Anyways, I did have a great time, but really not much happened… But just a few months later, I get a call from Cathy… "Hey, it's been like three years…" The last time we saw each other, I was still working at the Consulate in Guangzhou. At that time, I was in the second semester of the doctoral program on Jungian psychology and we had been studying the concept of synchronicity… And the way we ran into each other that time was a textbook example of the concept…

What is Synchronizität?

Synchronicity (German: Synchronizität) is a concept, first introduced by Carl Jung, in which he holds that events are "meaningful coincidences" if they occur with no causal relationship yet seem to be meaningfully related. During his career, Jung furnished several different definitions of synchronicity. He termed it as an "acausal connecting (togetherness) principle," also called it "meaningful coincidence," and defined it as a kind of "acausal parallelism." He introduced the concept in the early 1920s but only gave a full statement of it in 1951 in an Eranos lecture.

In 1952, Jung published a paper "Synchronizität als ein Prinzip akausaler Zusammenhänge" (Synchronicity – An Acausal Connecting Principle) in a volume which also contained a related study by the physicist and Nobel laureate Wolfgang Pauli, who was sometimes critical of Jung's ideas. Jung's argued that just as events may be connected by causality through physicality, they may also be connected by "meaning." Events connected by meaning need not have an explanation in terms of causality, thus synchronicity can "work" and not contradict the Axiom of Causality.

Jung courted controversy by using the concept in arguing for the existence of the paranormal. In the introduction to his 19XX book, *Jung on Synchronicity and the Paranormal*, Roderick Main wrote: "The culmination of Jung's lifelong engagement with the paranormal is his theory of synchronicity, the view that the structure of reality includes a principle of acausal connection which manifests itself most conspicuously in the form of meaningful coincidences. Difficult, flawed, prone to misrepresentation, this theory nonetheless remains one of the most suggestive attempts yet made to bring the paranormal within the bounds of intelligibility. It has been found relevant by psychotherapists, parapsychologists, researchers of spiritual experience and a growing number of non-specialists. Indeed, Jung's writings in this area form an excellent general introduction to the whole field of the paranormal."

In *Synchronicity: An Acausal Connecting Principle*, Jung makes the case for the paranormal quite explicitly: "...it is impossible, with our present resources, to explain ESP, or the fact of meaningful coincidence, as a phenomenon of energy. This makes an end of the causal explanation as well, for 'effect' cannot be understood as anything except a phenomenon of energy. Therefore it cannot be a question of cause and effect, but of a falling together in time, a kind of simultaneity. Because of this quality of simultaneity, I have picked on the term 'synchronicity' to designate a hypothetical factor equal in rank to causality as a principle of explanation."

Synchronicity was a principle which, Jung felt, gave conclusive evidence for his concepts of Archetypes and the Collective Unconscious.

Jung foresaw it as a governing principle underlying the whole of human social, emotional, psychological, and spiritual experience and history. By embracing the emergence of a synchronistic paradigm, Jung thought, we can make a significant move away from Cartesian dualism, and the dead end of materialistic "Scientism."

However, even as Jung presented his work on synchronicity in 1951 at the Eranos Conference, his ideas on synchronicity were still evolving. On Feb. 25, 1953, in a letter to Carl Seelig, the Swiss journalist and biographer of Albert Einstein, Jung wrote, "Professor Einstein was my guest on several occasions at dinner... These were very early days when Einstein was developing his first theory of relativity. It was he who first started me on thinking about a possible relativity of time as well as space, and their psychic conditionality. More than 30 years later the stimulus led to my relation with the physicist professor W. Pauli and to my thesis of psychic synchronicity."

Following in-depth discussions with Albert Einstein and Wolfgang Pauli, Jung believed there were parallels between synchronicity and aspects of relativity theory and quantum mechanics. Jung came to believe life was not a series of random events but rather an expression of a deeper order, which he and Pauli referred to as "Unus mundus." Their "discovery" of this deeper order led to their insight that Man was embedded in "universal wholeness." They further realized that "awakening" that one is a part of this wholeness has to be more than an intellectual belief, but must also encompass elements of spiritual awakening.

From the traditional religious perspective, synchronicity shares similar characteristics of an "intervention of grace." Jung found that in a person's life, synchronicity served a role similar to that of meaningful dreams that serve the purpose of shifting a person's egocentric conscious thinking to greater wholeness, to see connections and opportunities (or dangers) that a purely material perspective would disallow as a "mere coincidence." Arthur Koestler's 1972 book, The Roots of Coincidence, makes a strong argument that synchronicity and the paranormal are aspects of a deeper universal principle. Of course, the idea of synchronicity as extending beyond mere coincidence or that it offers proof of paranormal events is widely rejected in the academic and scientific communities. In his time, Jung was widely dismissed by other psychologists as having become a "mystic" in his later years.

I define synchronicity as the universe "synchronizing" space-time phenomena to deliver a message. What one does with that message, however, is not up to the universe, but rather the receiver of the message. I imagine that the universe is actually much more "littered" with "synchronicity" events, but most of them go unobserved by their intended recipients. I also imagine that the universe is relentless and that synchronicity will always find a way to get the message through...

So... briefly, here is what happened in Guangzhou that Sunday afternoon. I am sitting in a hotel coffee shop waiting for some friends and I was musing about how synchronicity might have worked in my own life and remembering how many coincidences had to happen for Cathy and me to meet for the first time on that plane in Beijing when, just then, I get a text from Cathy... At that time, it had been a couple years since we even emailed, so I was surprised. The text tells me that she is in town... with her mother... one week business trip... am I still in Guangzhou? Well, not much longer, but I am glad to catch up with "the one that got away" before I head back to DC...

As I prepare to text back, I lift my head up from the phone, I see Cathy and a large group of people at a table on the other side of the lobby!

Then it hits me. I was just thinking about her. I was just thinking about how synchronicity played a role in how we first met. Now, she just texted me after (?) years. Now I look up and she's over there. Now, that is synchronicity.

I make use of this synchronous event to make a good impression on my future mother-in-law and her group of friends by taking them out a few times and showing them around town, but at the time, I had no idea if we would ever see each other again or not as I was ending my tour in China and might not be back for years. But It just seemed like the right and polite thing to do.

Soon after this chance meeting, I left China and started working at "Main State," the Department HQ in Washington, DC. After about a year there I resigned from the Foreign Service. About a year after that I go to Haifa. During these years, Cathy and I don't talk or email as there was just no intersection in our lives, but just a few months after I come back from Mount Carmel, I find myself on a late night phone call with her that somehow turns to we should "really be together, and not split up anymore…"

This time, I get the message loud and clear. Strange and highly synchronous events follow and after getting permission from her parents, and meeting many of her relatives on a whirlwind tour of China, we find ourselves at the San Francisco Bahá'í Center, preparing to recite the Bahá'í marriage vows "We will all, verily, abide by the Will of God."

The Bahá'í marriage ceremony is done differently in each culture and there are very little required ceremonies. The only compulsory part of the wedding is the reading of the wedding vows prescribed by Bahá'u'lláh which both the groom and the bride recite.

It occurred to me the wedding vow is the plural form of "I will to will Thy Will"…

Now I understand there is a kind of demonstration of fidelity that can only happen in a marriage of equal partners, who like two wings of one bird, together fly in the shared heavens of a mutual love. Yeah, it can be like that…

And that is my story about how we got married.

Chapter Six

GO BEYOND BELIEF

Psychic Powers

I admire and have sympathy for the "natural" psychics. From everything I have learned there are such people and it can't be an easy life for them. Marla Frees comes to mind… I met Marla at a Tom Campbell MBT conference. She seemed like a very warm and receptive person. At the time I did not know she was, "the" Marla Frees.

The inexplicable gift of communicating with the "other side" came without warning while Marla was shooting a TV commercial in Los Angeles. All of a sudden, Marla felt she was given a message. The father of the actor sitting across from her wanted the actor to know he was "happy about the new baby." The message came to her from the father… who was deceased!

Not sure how he would react, Marla took a chance and told him. The actor was shocked. Marla was gob-smacked herself. But, more and more messages from deceased loved ones and a powerful psychic awareness demanded her attention, and Marla followed her heart. She quit acting, and never looked back. Marla is now a full-time psychic who uses her gifts to help families from all over the country heal by connecting with loved ones beyond the vale.

As Marla tells her story in the autobiography "American Psychic," her spiritual journey began as a small-town girl who learns to develop her psychic gifts through a personal relationship with God, leading her on a synchronistic path that weaves through the trauma of her childhood, the drama of her acting career, and once, she awakened to her psychic gift, amazing adventures in healing and transformation. Along the way, she tells of how she explored her abilities with US military "psychic spies," assisted detectives on homicide cases, and delved into the science behind her abilities with Tom Campbell. Marla has learned to trust the voice of "Spirit," which never fails her. Marla's story is one of spiritual transformation and her journey to realms that are as astonishing as they are inspiring.

Some will find healing in Marla's work; others will see fiction. Think what you like, and make of it what you will…

As for me, even with my various out-of-body adventures, I do not consider myself a "psychic." I feel that what I do, anyone can do, and my wife does it much better. I don't consider remote viewing, OBEs and even precognition or clairvoyance to be enough to warrant the label of a scientifically verifiable "PSI" event. As a Jungian, all of these can be explained as an internal, albeit highly synchronistic event. I have to reserve this rarified level for what parapsychologists call "Macro-PK." This term denotes psychokinetic (PK) effects that, like table turning, are large enough to be observed by the naked eye. In contrast, Micro-PK refers to psychokinetic effects so minute that they require statistical analysis or special methods to detect.

As for my UFO and Close Encounter experiences, I remain open-minded. I still hold that without additional evidence, the experiences can still be explained as purely internal mental phenomena as well as the other extreme of physical beings in technologically advanced crafts that are beyond our understanding. At this point, I don't need certainty. I have learned that the answers that I get from OBEs relate more to my psychic and spiritual questions. I now know the things that I need to know, I always knew… within.

When Jung was interviewed shortly before his death, he was asked, "do you believe in God?".

After a long pause, Jung replied, "I don't have to believe… I know!"

I can't bend spoons with my mind and don't need to. I can't read people's minds and I am pretty glad about that. There is a part of me that "worries" I could, and "I" am nowhere near ready to handle that kind of power. Manipulate the weather with your mind. Stop someone's heart with a thought. Spy on anyone anywhere anytime... Could you stop yourself?

Are these the chains of thought that scare people away from parapsychology? But fear not, these are well-trodden paths. History is replete with stories of people who had such powers and more, but it never quite works out...

In Dr. Jeffrey Mishlove's book, *The PK Man, the true and strange story of Ted Owens*, he tells us of his 10-year study of Owens and his observation of the incredible feats of powerful psychokinetism apparently caused by Owens. Ted Owens (reminiscent of George Van Tassel) consistently claimed that his abilities were given to him by "Space Intelligences." Owens, who had a genius-level IQ and was a member of Mensa, believed he had been subject to "psychic surgery" by "space intelligences" to alter his brain in order to allow him to receive their telepathic messages.

He considered himself a "UFO prophet" and compared himself with Moses, claiming psychokinetic powers that enabled him to not only predict but control lightning, hurricanes, tornadoes, earthquakes and volcanoes. Dubbing himself the "PK Man", Owens professed that his alleged powers were given to him by space intelligences who wished to call attention to the dangers that nuclear weapons and environmental pollution posed for mankind.

Acceptance of the bizarre and extreme nature of the claims proved too difficult for many. Science fiction and comic book writer Otto Binder wrote that Owens suffered a series of accidents resulting in brain trauma, which he felt were responsible for Owens' belief in his supposed powers. Mishlove describes how when his claims were ignored or challenged, Owens would threaten to use his powers to produce earthquakes, civil unrest, UFO sightings, strange weather events, and other powerful phenomena to "prove" they were real. Often the events would happen nearly precisely as Owens predicted, or "caused," as he would say. Owens even stated of his intent to down aircraft to garner attention, and in one instance commented that he might have done so inadvertently once by carelessly drawing down a lightning strike.

Mishlove maintains doubts as to the truth to Owens' abilities, but argues that to cast Owens aside as a fraud with a knack for picking the times and places of catastrophes would be a mistake. By thoroughly analyzing volumes of correspondence, interviews, and newspaper reports on Owens as well as by directly communicating with "the world's greatest psychic," as Owens liked to claim to be, Mishlove offers a balanced and critical view of a man who could be a disingenuous con-man, or an unbalanced PK-master who used his powers for petty acts of revenge.

I have long felt that psychic abilities of the magnitude claimed by the PK Man are possible, but not suitable for people who have not learned to "let go of their ego." Ted Owens is only a recent example from a long line of people who suffered ego-inflation as the result of suddenly acquiring what they perceive as tremendous power. Lottery winners at worse can hurt themselves, but an ego-driven PK-master out of control can, theoretically, hurt anyone and everyone...

Who needs HAARP to control the weather?

Because I was born in the year of the dragon, I was fond of stories where friendly dragons were assigned the task of maintaining good weather for humanity by the Jade Emperor. In children's fantasies where a dragon and a human would fall in love and have a baby, one of the signs that the kid was "special" was that he or she would control the weather with their emotional state. In the stories there is always a disaster before the kid learns to control the power.

I identified with that special kid character and imagined I could control the weather. I knew better than to tell anyone I had such a conceited idea, but I enjoyed any coincidental times when the weather would correspond to my wishing. I never gave this mental game much thought, but then there was that time when I went camping, and I called out loud for more thunder and it kept coming like six or seven times... Or that time I was mad at my friend and in a light drizzle a clap of thunder exploded behind him and almost knocked him to the ground... and I kinda knew it was coming...

When "We Are the World," a song written by Michael Jackson and Lionel Richie and produced by Quincy Jones came out, I had just turned 21 and was going to college. Following the success of Band Aid's 1984 "Do They Know It's Christmas?" project in the United Kingdom, the American benefit single for relief of African famine due to drought brought together some of the most famous artists in the music industry at the time. The song was released on March 7, 1985. I really liked that song and I thought they sure could use some rain...

I listened to that song and did a crazy rain dance in my living room... just for fun... to let off some steam... I forgot all about it... A couple days go by...

Back then there was no 24-hour news, no internet news feed, not even mobile phones. You had three networks and half an hour of new at dinner time. I sometimes watch, sometimes don't. This night, I am half-watching over dinner... eating a TV dinner... "More freak rainstorms inundate Addis Ababa International Airport even as drought continues to grip the rest of the country. Overnight additional storms are predicted while crews rush to move tons of relief supplies recently delivered and now feared will be left to rot as water damage looks certain..."

I let that sink in over a bite of Salisbury steak... No... There is NO WAY that had anything to do with me...

Just in case, I stopped trying to wish for a nicer day. I just let the weather do whatever the weather does... People seem to prefer stories where there is an easy "origins" proposed for the granting of a special power, but I don't have one, nor do I claim any special powers. But if I did, would saying it comes from a higher power, so I am not the one responsible, make it easier to use that power?

If people like Van Tassel and Owens are manifesting innate psychic powers and not being visited by "space intelligences," the implications for the rest of us are staggering! It could mean that human being are potentially all capable of inventing amazing machines from innate knowledge, using macro-PK, and who knows what else. No aliens or God needed...

When I was first learning about the Bahá'í Faith, I asked my friend, "What do the teachings say about psychic powers, contacting the dead and things like that?" Some miraculous feats are presumed to be linked with the development of latent psychic faculties in man. Abdu'l-Bahá, the Beloved Master of the Bahá'í Faith, admits the reality of the "super normal" psychic faculties, but deprecates any attempt to force their premature development. "To tamper with psychic forces while in this world interferes with the condition of the soul in the world to come. These forces are real, but, normally, are not active on this plane."

Abdu'l-Bahá uses the example of a child in the womb to explain the idea. The child has eyes, ears, hands, feet, etc., but they are not used in activity. Only once the child is born in the material world, do these organs become active. Similarly, psychic powers are not to be used in this world, and it is dangerous to cultivate them here.

"That makes a lot of sense, so can a departed soul contact someone still on earth?" I asked.

Abdu'l-Bahá once answered this question, he said, "A conversation can be held, but not as our conversation. There is no doubt that the forces of the higher worlds interplay with the forces of this plane. The heart of man is open to inspiration; this is spiritual communication. As in a dream one talks with a friend while the mouth is silent, so is it in the conversation of the spirit. A man may converse with the ego within him saying: "May I do this? Would it be advisable for me to do this work?" Such as this is conversation with the higher self."

However, Abdu'l-Bahá points out that there can be, under certain rare circumstances, such as those experienced by the prophets, communion with some soul gone before into the invisible world. Most other experiences of this type that people claim to have with departed souls are the product of their imaginations – however real they may seem to them to be.

The whole purpose of life in the material world is the coming forth into the world of reality where psychic forces will become active. To live properly is to prepare for the next world properly. Practices such as intercourse with spirits of the departed, telepathy, etc., ought not to be indulged in either for curiosity or for their own sake, and might be potentially harmful.

Shoghi Effendi, called the Guardian by Bahá'ís, explains that such powers" should be left dormant, and not exploited, even when we do so with the sincere belief we are helping others. We do not understand their nature and have no way of being sure of what is true and what is false in such matters." He adds, "If children are inclined to be psychic they should not be blamed for it too harshly; they should not be encouraged to strengthen their powers in this direction." In most cases, psychic phenomena indicate deep psychological disturbance, and we should avoid giving undue consideration to such matters.

"So, what about prophetic dreams and visions of the future, can these be real?"

The Guardian says that it is very difficult to distinguish truth from imagination. However, he explained that, "True visions…can be granted to those who are spiritually pure and receptive, and are not therefore confined to the Prophets alone."

"Okay… next question, why is there so much evil in the world?" We did that over many lunches and a few dinners for weeks on end…

My friend's explanation of the teachings rang true to my experience. Psychic powers are real, but not meant for this world. If we force their use prematurely we end up hurting ourselves and the people around us. It strengthened my admiration of the teachings…

I sincerely agreed with the Guardian that such powers "…should be left dormant, and not exploited, even when we do so with the sincere belief we are helping others. We do not understand their nature and have no way of being sure of what is true and what is false in such matters." While I never allowed myself to fully believe I could influence the weather despite the "freak rainstorm over Addis Ababa" thing, I intentionally stopped "wishing" for nice weather. Just in case… That whole butterfly effect thing…

However, a few years later after I had declared as a Bahá'í, while I was being driving across eastern Taiwan during a typhoon, I "used" my power. I had been invited by a prominent Buddhist group on a personal visit to their newly completed temple, and the driver they sent insisted on trying to get there on schedule despite the coming storm. Perhaps due to my status at the time as a US Consul in Hong Kong, the group sent a driver and another escort who acted like he was my bodyguard or something. If you know eastern Taiwan, you will know it is a lot like the California coast at places a narrow two-lane road with a steep rock face on one side and a sharp cliff on the other. Known for earthquakes and landslides and hot springs from being on the "Ring of Fire," Eastern Taiwan is also very exposed to Pacific typhoons. The brave driver handled the weather, but we were nearly the only car still on the road.

I thought, "If I can actually do anything with weather, now is the time to do it," and I prayed for the typhoon to move out to sea for as long as possible while we drove on...

After a short while, the rain decreases noticeably...

We stop at a restaurant to take advantage of the pause in the storm and watch the weather report while we eat... the live satellite footage shows the typhoon just did a big bend away from Taiwan and is headed towards the Philippines... We are almost there so, I "pray" to take back any undue influence on my part...

Back on the road, I soon recognize that the driver and the "bodyguard" have been subtly trying to convert me to their school of Buddhism. They don't disparage my choice nor frankly know anything about the Bahá'í Faith, but make clear their belief that their master, the "Living Buddha," is the way of truth for all people. I don't find their arguments convincing in the least, but it does kick off an internal dialogue on the nature of knowing I stop listening to their inane examples of their master's miracles. " even the fish saluted when he walked by this lake "

The car fades away as I close my eyes and listen to the rain talk, and reflect on how do we recognize truth? What if these guys are right and their master is some kind of higher consciousness as I believe Bahá'u'lláh to be, but alive today, and I am missing it?

My mind offers up an interesting proposition. If Bahá'u'lláh is speaking the truth, you could ask for proof of some kind right now. What kind of proof? Some sign that only I would appreciate? As I ponder this question, the rain is once again unrelentingly pounding the roof of the car. The typhoon came back. We drive on in silence after they run out of miracles. The rain is so loud it's hard to talk anyway. As we pull up to the hotel, the rain is so heavy it is hard to see the driveway, and the bodyguard guy gets ready to pull out his umbrella The car comes to a stop and the guy opens his door and looks up

I open my door and notice there is a hole in the clouds above us. The rain has completely stopped in a moment, just as if someone turned off a spigot. The hole is big enough that we can see the stars. I think to myself, that can't be the eye of the typhoon? We all stand there for a few second marveling at the sudden cessation of the downpour.

I didn't link this event to what I had just been thinking about earlier at that moment (missing the synchronicity of the message), and just waved good night and headed inside the hotel. As soon as I got under the awning at the entrance, the rain starts pouring again like someone turned back on a spigot. Now I made the connection and I saw the sign. But did God really bother to stop the rain to give me a sign or did I "cause" that? Or was it as some Jungians would be tempted to say, high synchronistic, but nothing supernatural here…

Can I have option four, all of the above?

In my first book, my idea was to help people who are fearful of looking into their spiritual nature find a step-by-step way to overcome that fear. To face the fear of the unknown – the biggest one being death. In this book, the goal was to help people see that all belief systems, whether ones foisted on us by the social status systems we grow up in or the ones we choose for ourselves are ultimately just that, beliefs. I have attempted to show we are not limited to who we are today. Fear is the first limit. Unfounded beliefs that block access to actual experience are much worse.

Belief trumps evidence

As Sadhguru says, only what we experience is true for us. Beliefs could be true or not true. If we forget that and defend our beliefs as if they are our actual experiences, we are taking a big risk. If we are lucky and the belief is true, you will move towards truth. If it is just a belief and not true, you will still defend it as "truth" and even destroy any opposing facts and evidence that threatens it.

If parapsychology is attacked for being lacking in scientific evidence, mainstream science in the form of archaeology and paleontology should be attacked for making up, suppressing and even destroying evidence. The "Piltdown Man" is a famous hoax in which bone fragments were presented as the fossilized remains of a previously unknown early human.

In 1912, the amateur archaeologist Charles Dawson claimed that he had discovered the "missing link" between ape and man. After finding a section of a human-like skull in Pleistocene gravel beds near Piltdown, East Sussex, Dawson contacted Arthur Smith Woodward, Keeper of Geology at the Natural History Museum. Dawson and Smith Woodward "discovered" more bones and artifacts at the site, which they connected to the same individual. These included a jawbone, more skull fragments, a set of teeth, and primitive tools.

Smith Woodward reconstructed the skull fragments and "hypothesized" that they belonged to a human ancestor from 500,000 years ago. The discovery was announced at a Geological Society meeting and Dawson "humbly" chose to give the "new find" the Latin name *Eoanthropus dawsoni* ("Dawson's dawn-man").

A full 41 years were to pass before the assemblage of bones was conclusively exposed in 1953 as a forgery. It was found to have consisted of the altered mandible and some teeth of an orangutan deliberately combined with the cranium of a fully developed, though small-brained, modern human. The Piltdown hoax ended up generating more attention to the subject of human evolution, and while the fraud was done to support Darwin's theory of evolution, its exposure strangely did little to slow the stampede in the public mind that sooner or later, the real missing link will be found.

110 years and counting...

Now consider the case of Ralph Glidden. In 1896, Glidden was a 15-year-old boy who had just moved with his family to Catalina Island, the largest of the Channel Islands off southern California. The teen soon developed a burgeoning interest in the various Indian artifacts and "midden" burial sites to be found scattered about the Channel Islands after he purportedly stubbed his toe on a human skull while looking for pearls on San Nicolas Island. He reportedly became obsessed with such things and became an amateur archeologist, going on to organize numerous excavations to uncover ancient burial sites on Catalina Island between the years of 1919 and 1928.

During these excursions he uncovered an alleged 800 secret burial sites around the island and a myriad of Indian artifacts and relics, as well as thousands of ancient Native remains, which he sold to museums and collectors. When William Wrigley, Jr., the chewing gum magnate, bought the land rights to the island in the 1920s, he ordered that all such finds would be the exclusive property of the Field Museum of Natural History of Chicago. The Heye Foundation, working under the National Museum of the American Indian in New York City, itself a part of the Smithsonian Institution, was contracted by the museum to carry out all excavations on Catalina Island, and Glidden was given a top spot in this pursuit due to his unique local knowledge.

Unfortunately for Glidden, in 1924 after most of the finds were transferred out, the foundation cut all funding, and he was forced to keep his head above water by opening a ramshackle museum for his few remaining finds in the town of Avalon, on Catalina Island, which he called the "Catalina Museum of Island Indians." The whole museum was a rather grim and gruesome affair, utilizing old skeletons as decorations. It could all be seen in retrospect as rather exploitative, turning priceless treasures from the past into macabre exhibitions for the curious, and making money off of them, but by all accounts Glidden was actually quite serious about the scientific pursuit of archaeology, and in those days this sort of behavior was sort of par for the course concerning ancient artifacts.

Among all of the curious discoveries made by Glidden, the most bizarre was his claim that he had uncovered a race of giants who had once inhabited the island. He came forward to announce that during his excavations he had come across several skeletons across the island that were far larger than normal humans, measuring an alleged 7 to 9 feet tall. Bizarrely, this would turn out to be not the only claim of such amazing finds among the Channel Islands.

Apparently in 1913, a German named Dr. A.W Furstenan had found the skeleton of what appeared to be an 8-foot tall human on Catalina Island, which was found amongst other artifacts including a flat stone bearing odd, unidentifiable symbols. This particular skeleton was allegedly found in Avalon Bay in hard black sand, and it reportedly mostly disintegrated when it was brought to the surface and exposed to air, leaving only the skull, jawbone, and a foot intact. There was also a later report of a dig on nearby Santa Rosa Island that in 1959 supposedly unearthed several 7-foot-tall skeletons with skulls painted red which had double rows of teeth and six fingers and toes instead of five. Interestingly, double rows of teeth were apparently a common feature among the human remains found in the Channel Islands.

Another of the Channel Islands, San Nicolas Island, was also the scene of numerous findings of larger-than-average human remains, which were surmised to be a different race from the more normal-sized inhabitants. Glidden concocted a theory that the islands had once been inhabited by a race of fair-skinned, blue-eyed giants, with the average height of a full-grown male estimated at around 7 feet.

The claim of course generated widespread media interest, but the main problem with Glidden's fantastic "discoveries" is that there is very little record of where they went after they were apparently sent to the University of California and the Smithsonian. These institutions have repeatedly denied that any such specimens are in their collections. There were those who came forward over the years to say that they had personally seen the skeletons, but these stories are circumstantial at best.

It has been speculated that the bones are locked away in top secret vaults along with the field reports and photos to go with them. Regardless of whether any of this is true or not, none of the alleged skeletons has ever been officially released as evidence for examination and it is unclear what happened to all of these remains that were shipped off to... what remains?

Similar cases of discoveries going into academic black holes are not uncommon. If a certain belief system has a strong enough hold on you, you will rather make up, suppress or destroy evidence that threatens it. Careers have been sidelined or ruined due to "unbelievable" findings.

Now consider the life of Professor Beverly Rubik. Dr. Rubik earned her PhD in biophysics in 1979 at the University of California at Berkeley. As a frontier scientist, she is now internationally renowned as an early explorer of "biofield" science and energy medicine. But earlier in her career these interests negatively affected her access to grants and caused her to be declined tenured at one university.

Biofield was not considered a "real" area of research and only after much difficulty was Dr. Rubik able to create the Institute for Frontier Science (IFS) in 1996 with the help of private donations. By 2002, public acceptance of the biofield was growing and IFS was awarded a National Institute of Health grant for "frontier medicine" research on Biofield science in consortium with researchers at the University of Arizona. Dr. Rubik was a project director and supervised studies on *reiki*, a form of Japanese spiritual healing, and on *qigong* therapy, a healing practice that originated in China.

If we as a society can overcome our fear, and separate ourselves from inherited belief systems to embrace experience, what will become possible for the more gifted individuals within it?

What is the maximum human potential? There are plenty of stories in science fiction where "some guy" is just born with superhuman power for no apparent reason. Usually the nature of the power helps the hero overcome his fear and any false beliefs, but he tends to always get stuck on... himself. His ego is his worst enemy.

This story has been played out many times in science fiction, but let me share a "true" story that was told to me... it sounds like science fiction, but who knows?

In the first book I mentioned published reports from China that claimed to document experiments that proved teleportation of various objects by human psychics, and the reaction of a noted US scientist that he believed the reports are authentic. My qigong teacher told me he heard stories about what these experiments ultimately led to and why they ended...

According to the stories... The best "psychic-teleporters" from the early trials were recruited and given special training to increase their abilities with the idea of somehow weaponizing the skill. The most talented one proves the most difficult to manage and during an argument, he teleports his commander into a nearby lake. When the military police go to arrest him, he is not to be found on the base. Six months later, Chinese intelligence locates him in Las Vegas, Nevada. The stories end with different versions, in some he is recruited by US intelligence, in others, he returns to China and is convinced to join an elite group of psychic spies. In every version, he skips out again, dooming the program to failure since no government can tolerate a weapon it cannot control. Hey, the whole thing sounds pretty unbelievable, but perhaps unbelievable stories are one of "truth's protective layers…"

Personal Interlude

In my very first year overseas with the Foreign Service I was tasked with visiting an American citizen who had been in a coma for a month in a hospital near Taichung in Central Taiwan. This young woman had been found by the side of the road. Police suspect she was the victim of a hit-and-run. She had no identification on her and they have not been able to locate anyone who could help contact her family. I did the required checklist items. No passport? No contacts in US? I write down the contact numbers at the hospital for her case, and before I leave I hold her hand for a long moment. The Taiwanese staff looks at me a bit funny and I am not sure why I did it. She's so alone here… Wish there was more I could do… I go back and write up the report.

The very next day, we get a call from the hospital. That girl woke up and they already contacted her family. She's going to be fine.

Did I help to wake her up? Do I have healing hands? I play with fantasies that I am a great healer, admired for my powers… then the fantasy turns to… then I would have to change my life, and deal with all the sick people… I don't even want to fantasize about that… because it's all about me and what I want, of course…

Three years later, as my father is dying, I remembered the fantasy… I am a psychic healer…

I used whatever power was in me to try to heal him. I prayed. When there was no one to look on, I laid my hands on him, with the most sincere healing intent. Nothing happened.

I am such an egotistical idiot... Did I really think I could heal someone with touching them?

There's going to be a "family meeting" tomorrow to decide if we keep dad on the ventilator...

I walk around the hospital ward aimlessly. My mind numbed from too much emotion...

I overhear two of the nurses talking... The younger one is commenting on someone...

"...that Mr. Yen is still holding on after three weeks... I mean usually patients in his condition don't even last a few days, right?"

The older nurse looks up at her young colleague, "Yeah, it's a bit of a miracle..."

Conclusion

BOBA AND PYRAMIDS

I tried Boba tea for the first time when I arrived in Taiwan in July of 1990. It tasted like good Hong Kong-style sweet milk tea with big tapioca balls on the bottom. You use an extra wide straw to suck up the little gel balls. The story was that it was invented when a Taichung teashop owner accidentally spilled her tapioca pudding into her milk tea then realized it was a match made in sweet drink heaven. I thought it was okay but had no idea it was going to get so popular in the coming decades. I would drink it intermittently over the years, but sweet drinks were never really my thing. Years later, long after my Close Encounter of the WTF Kind and the head-poking woman's cryptic remark about eating some kind of "gel" to help my brain, I had a strange flash of recognition when I had a Boba tea after a long break from it.

As I sucked down the round gelatinous balls of tapioca, or cassava to be precise, the thought hit me that this was what she was talking about. My intellectual mind could not make a connection, but I trusted the feeling enough to immediately try to find out more about something that I realized I knew very little about.

Cassava (Manihot esculenta subsp. esculenta) is a staple crop with great economic importance worldwide, yet its evolutionary and geographical origins have remained unresolved and controversial. Recently plant geneticists have investigated this crop's domestication in a phylogeographic study based on the use of single-copy nuclear gene

3-phosphate technique (G3pdh). The G3pdh test provides high levels of noncoding sequence variation in cassava and its wild relatives, with 28 haplotypes identified among 212 individuals examined. The test data represents one of the first uses of a single-copy nuclear gene in a plant phylogeographic study and yielded several important insights into cassava's evolutionary origin:

One, cassava was likely domesticated from wild populations along the southern border of the Amazon basin.

Two, cassava does not seem to be derived from several progenitor species, as previously proposed.

Three, cassava does not share haplotypes with Manihot pruinosa, a closely related, potentially hybridizing species.

These findings offered little light on the picture of cassava's origin except to rule out existing theories.

Cassava leaves are used as an herbal remedy. The root of the plant is what is used to make tapioca, the starch used in making the gel balls in milk tea. Taking refined cassava in dietary supplement form is said to offer a variety of health benefits including enhanced fertility. Until recently, when numerous studies unveiled the health benefits of this versatile root tuber, people regarded cassava as a poor man's food. Some are now considering it a "super food" due to health benefits that include aiding digestion, lowering blood cholesterol, lowering blood sugar, preventing cancer, and boosting immunity. But the health effect I found most interesting was cassava's supposed role in limiting neural damage in the brain and preventing Alzheimer's disease.

Cassava contains cyanide and has to be prepared in an elaborate manner before it can be safely eaten. Like the plant itself, the way to properly prepare it, is believed to be a gift of the "gods" in most indigenous societies where cassava is part of the diet. Cassava was the staple food and principal crop of the Tainos (the indigenous tribe of the Caribbean). It was so important to their survival that the Tainos referred to their homes as "Yucayeques", meaning the place where yucca is grown. The Tainos held the plant in such great esteem that the tribe, including the Chief (Cacique), all took part in yucca's respectful cultivation. They would maintain large pots of boiling cassava juice where seasonal vegetables, meat and fish were added. The resulting stew could be added to or consumed at any time. This procedure was the origin of the "pepper pot" which to this day is traditional food in many parts of the Caribbean. The Taino also processed yucca into cassava bread, called casaba, for long-term storage

The cassava plant appears in many ancient stories. In one mythology, the supreme deity of the Tainos, Yucahu, god of the sea, and his mother, Atabey, the goddess of fresh water and human fertility, give the yucca to the people and teach them the secret of how to prepare it. In another Taino epic, it is the human hero named Deminan who, with his brothers, stole the cassava from the gods and brought it to the Tainos. These stories mirror other mythologies throughout Latin America where cassava is gifted or wrested from supernatural beings. This myth was referenced and recreated when the Tainos buried stone carvings of Yucahu in agricultural fields. The stones were triangular in shape and resembled a sprouting cassava tuber.

I had no idea that there was such an interesting story behind the little gel balls in my Boba tea! As a fun food experiment, I found a good organic supply and started using different preparations to consume this "sacred" food in the way that traditional societies would have by and for a time replaced almost all my carbohydrate intake such as rice or bread with cassava. Frankly, it is a very bland product that I would not willingly choose it as a big part of my diet if it were not for an experiment. After going through pounds and pounds of it over a few weeks, I felt I had had enough. I didn't feel any difference. Certainly I didn't notice my brain being "bigger" or otherwise affected in any way. Regardless, I felt my hangup regarding the cryptic remark had been resolved. I found the "gel" and I ate it the way it was supposed to be eaten, and nothing...

Shortly after I completed my "brain food" experiment, I had a lucid dream while taking a nap in the afternoon. This happened about six months before my wife's UFO encounter, so I had not had any experience with OBEs yet. The dream begins as a rather normal flying dream, but almost immediately I become lucid and start deciding which direction to go. I soon see a golden pyramid in the distance and head towards it. As I get closer I see the entire valley that the pyramid overlooks is beautifully landscaped. There are other smaller pyramids on the other end of the valley and a river flows through the middle of it. The entire area looks manicured to very fine detail but as I fly over the valley I don't see any inhabitants. There are various lights attached to the sides of the valley and on the pyramids making the scene reminiscent of a sparkly paradise. I noticed gold was used to cover many of the buildings and large parts of the pyramids.

"This must be some alien planet," I think to myself as I fly towards the largest pyramid. Without meaning to I cross over the tip of the pyramid and feel myself magnetized in mid-air about fifty feet over it. Enormous energies rush through me and it is… rather pleasant. I am in no hurry to go anywhere and I decide to just "plug in" and stay there… I wake up very refreshed.

A few weeks later I am watching a video on the Bosnian Pyramids and I recognized the scene from the dream. I replay the part of the video that features a flyover of the Visoko Valley. The now overgrown pyramids can still be made out where the Bosna River and Fojnica River merge and flow into the valley. The video was made to debunk the claims made by Samir Osmanagich, the Bosnian who discovered the pyramid in 2005. Much is made about the repeated condemnation of Osmanagich by professional archaeologists in the video. Archaeologists who signed a statement issued by the European Association of Archaeologists Declaration protesting the continuing support by the Bosnian authorities for the "so-called 'pyramid' project" are interviewed. One states, "This scheme is a cruel hoax on an unsuspecting public and has no place in the world of genuine science." Another calls it a "waste of scarce resources that would be much better used in protecting the genuine archaeological heritage of Bosnia-Herzegovina which is being lost on a daily basis."

However, in a country still recovering from the 1992-95 genocidal war, in which some 100,000 people were killed and 2.2 million were driven from their homes (the majority of them Bosnian Muslims), Osmanagich's findings have found a surprisingly receptive audience. Bosnian officials including a prime minister and two presidents have embraced them, along with the Sarajevo-based news media and hundreds of thousands of ordinary Bosnians. Critics argue they are drawn to the promise of a glorious past and a more prosperous future for their battered country. Some go further and say the pyramid claims are examples of pseudo-archaeology pressed into the service of nationalism, and charge Osmanagich with deliberate fraud and reshaping the hills to make them look more like pyramids.

The fact that pyramid mania has descended upon Bosnia since October 2005, when Osmanagich announced his discovery, shows there are financial incentives involved. Souvenir stands peddle pyramid-themed T-shirts, wood carvings, piggy banks, clocks and flip-flops. Nearby eateries serve meals on pyramid-shaped plates and coffee comes with pyramid-emblazoned sugar packets. Whatever incentives locals might have to foster the belief of pyramids in Bosnia, reporters from the BBC, Associated Press, Agence France-Presse and ABC's Nightline all found enough evidence to merit giving the claim extensive coverage. Most of the reports present the "official scientific" explanation of "flatiron" rock formations being responsible, but Nightline's report noted that in 2009 thermal imaging had revealed the presence of regularly shaped, concrete blocks beneath parts of the valley floor.

More favorable coverage shows why Osmanagich has also received substantial private financial support in addition to official backing from the Bosnian government. The evidence is clear and convincing for anyone not locked into a belief system that ancient pyramids CANNOT be true. His Pyramid of the Sun Foundation in Sarajevo has garnered hundreds of thousands of dollars in public donations and thousands more from state-owned companies. After Malaysian Prime Minister Mahathir Mohamad toured Visoko in July 2006, more contributions poured in. Christian Schwarz-Schilling, the former high representative for the international community in Bosnia and Herzegovina, visited the site in July 2007, then declared that "I was surprised with what I saw before my eyes, and the fact that such structures exist in Bosnia and Herzegovina."

Since 2005, Osmanagich and his supporters have initiated a long-running campaign to unearth areas surrounding the main pyramid and the surrounding area. The quiet excavations have uncovered what appears to be an ancient pyramid complex. In an interview with Philip Coppens in Nexus magazine (May 2006), Osmanagich suggested that

179

they were most likely constructed by the Illyrians, who lived in the area from 12,000 BC to 500 BC. However, after further excavation revealed a vast tunnel network connecting the pyramids, he has since argued that the Visočica site is an example of cultures building on top of other cultures. In 2017 Osmanagich reported he has found fossil evidence that suggests the structures date back 34,000 years.

Continuing excavation has found that the tunnels connecting the pyramids from beneath the complex actually cover the entire valley and extend to points beyond. Osmanagich named this network the Ravne tunnels, and it was within this ancient man-made underground system, estimated to be at least 2.4 miles (3.8 km) long, where he found fossilized leaves that carbon dating shows to be from 34,000 years ago.

It was clear to me now what I saw in the dream I had shortly before seeing my first video about the Bosnian pyramids was not an alien planet. I had "seen" what the Bosnian Pyramid Complex looked like in its heyday. Was having the dream so soon after completing my food experiment with cassava related in some way? Certainly seeing the video right after having the dream was highly synchronous and significant.

In the last book of the trilogy, I plan to examine the question of how we, as individuals, can learn to "let go" of the ego, and how our overinflated ego is the curse of modern humans, and the greatest threat to all life on Earth. Ironically, even if we overcome our fear and our beliefs, we can't just stomp on the ego and call it good. The ego is not something to be overcome: it needs to be maintained with a sufficient level of self-confidence, and allowed to grow as the "operational" part of the total personality. You have to "let it go," so it will come back "freed."

The paradox seems to be that to use the "tool" of the ego with sufficient control to do certain things, the "Self" must undergo self-forgetfulness and enter into the tool to the degree that it "becomes" the tool. This is perhaps why it seems easier to ascribe miracles to God or some other external cause as a shield against ego inflation. But when the shield becomes a shell, it will trap you.

When I consider what is humanly possible, it seems to me that the upper end of human potential has not been set by the Creator. Our fear, our beliefs, and our ego are the limits. Remove these and each individual will be freed to flower in his and her own way. It will not be the same for everyone. Our strength as humanity is unity in our diversity. Our downfall is egotistical thinking – me, my group, my country, my religion.

There is in me a strong desire to see the Bosnian Pyramids for myself in physical reality. The feeling began as a vacation fantasy. Then it got stronger and I started planning it and researching the ways to do it... Now, I have discussed it with my wife and have convinced her we should do it... It is more than something I want to do... It is something I am drawn to do. I can sense my "higher self" cheering on. There is growing in me a certainty that by the time I finally get to that unbelievable place, I will have learned what I need to write the last book of this trilogy... Let Go The Ego

Epilogue

THE UNBELIEVABLE TRUTH

As I prepare the final draft of *Places Beyond Belief* for publication, I thought an epilogue discussing the Novel Coronavirus (COVID 19) might be appropriate, but I realized the event was too current for me to fully digest and discuss. Then I noticed a news item that would serve as the perfect tale to tie up this book on going beyond what we currently believe to find the truth.

Barely noticed by the mainstream media, the United States government, acting through the Navy, officially confirmed that previously leaked classified videos of naval aviators chasing various unidentified aerial phenomena (UAP) were genuine Navy material, and has now declassified them. Here is the full text:

Statement by the Department of Defense on
the Release of Historical Navy Videos
APRIL 27, 2020

The Department of Defense has authorized the release of three unclassified Navy videos, one taken in November 2004 and the other two in January 2015, which have been circulating in the public domain after unauthorized releases in 2007 and 2017. The U.S. Navy previously acknowledged that these videos circulating in the public domain were indeed Navy videos. After a thorough review, the department has determined that the authorized release of these unclassified videos does not reveal any sensitive capabilities or systems, and does not impinge on any subsequent investigations of military air space incursions by unidentified aerial phenomena. DOD is releasing the videos in order to clear up any misconceptions by the public on whether or not the footage that has been circulating was real, or whether or not there is more to the videos. The aerial phenomena observed in the videos remain characterized as "unidentified." The released videos can be found at the Naval Air Systems Command FOIA Reading Room: https://www. navair.navy.mil/foia/documents.

As usual, you pull one layer back, you get more layers. Reading between the lines you can see that the policy remains that anything that might "reveal any sensitive capabilities or systems," or "impinge on investigations of incursions by UAP" will remain classified with criminal penalties attached to their release. The fact that this statement was released in the midst of the media fixation on Covid 19 is, of course, no accident. Is this what did Neil Armstrong meant when he spoke of "truth's protective layers..."

In this book, I describe a lot of things that are quite unbelievable for a lot of people simply because there is very little in their experience to reference anything similar. Some might react with "nice fiction," and read it that way. However, if we stop investigating life's possibilities at the borders of what we currently believe to be the limit, where would that leave us? Permanently limited. And how do we determine where that border is? Based on what your parents believe? Based on what your peers believe? Based on what "everybody" believes?

It is imperative that we learn to go beyond that. Even if we overcome our fear of the unknown and dare to go beyond the threshold of the physical, how far and where we can go is circumscribed by the beliefs we bring with us.

There are places to go beyond belief... because there lies human destiny.